Broken & Redeemed

Broken and Redeemed, by my good friend John Jarman, is powerful and full of life-changing truth. John shares his journey to freedom with such vulnerability and authenticity. He shares his pain of being broken and the joy and gratitude of being redeemed in Christ. John's story will encourage and equip you in your own journey to freedom. I highly recommend this book to not only be read but experienced. It shows us the process of finding freedom through complete surrender."

—**Eric Boles,** President, The Game Changers Inc.,
www.thegamechangersinc.com

"In a culture that expects a former Marine and football coach to be brash and ever-strong, it is refreshing to find a sharing as vulnerable as John Jarman's *Broken and Redeemed.* Challenge, failing, and loss are expressed openly as the reader is invited to follow his path toward discipleship. Especially meaningful are the chapter reflection questions which invite us to enter into a personal examination. In preaching a message of surrender, John Jarman instructs us effectively in how to find true strength in faith."

—**Mary Beth Hynes,** Christian Religious Educator

"Compelling, thought-provoking, and challenging! This story brings home how people struggle to be functional, make connections, and make a difference in personal and professional relationships—even in the strangest, saddest, and most restrictive circumstances. Your spirituality/faith gets you through more than you think possible! I personally recommend this challenging book."

—**Dr. Mike Martin,** DDS

"I've known John Jarman for almost ten years. Over that time I have seen him navigate the pain and suffering of his youth with great humility and Holy Spirit-driven persistence. He has persevered through very difficult psychological and emotional landmines while at the same time navigating challenging life circumstances, desperate to get to the bottom of his life story. What a holy journey it has been! This raw and honest depiction is written in simple terms, easy for anyone to digest. Divinely inspired, a book worthy of your review, I couldn't be prouder of John and his autobiographical testimony."

—**Scotty Kessler,** Sports Ministry and Discipleship Leader, Honorary Doctor of Human Letters, Faith Seminary

"Author John Jarman takes us on a spiritual journey that is both touching and heartbreakingly honest. It's John's story of God's grace and unconditional love in the midst of difficult personal circumstances and unwise life choices. If it seems to hit too close to home at times, it's because it's our story also. Different circumstances and choices perhaps, but pointing to the universal condition of brokenness nevertheless. John's testimony can help the reader leave their brokenness behind and embrace the joy and freedom of redemption in Christ."

—**Greg Chantler,** Retired Pastor, Evangelical Covenant Church, and Author of *Home to Pleasant Pastures*

"*Broken and Redeemed* is a robust testimony to the unlimited power of God to change lives through the gospel of Jesus Christ. John's story reveals the overarching truth of the Bible, which is that there is no level of brokenness or pain that God cannot heal and redeem for His greater honor and glory. If you are looking for an inspirational story that is also a practical guide for growing your faith in Christ, then *Broken and Redeemed* is a must read for you!"

—**Dan Shaw,** Master of Divinity, Active Reserve Lieutenant Commander Navy Chaplain (Iraq War Veteran), Sr. Pastor Emmanuel Lutheran Church, Tacoma, WA

"John's story is compelling, from the hardships of his early years to the man he has become today. He lived in a world of hurt from early childhood. He was raised in a dysfunctional family and learned how to just get by. He survived poor choices until he found God and let Christ into his life. Here, he also faced many battles, but his deep faith and spirituality set an example from which we all can learn. This book provides a stepping stone to one's own spiritual journey."

—**Marilyn Tuohy,** Librarian, Retired

BROKEN
&
REDEEMED

Finding Freedom through Complete Surrender

JOHN JARMAN

NASHVILLE

NEW YORK • LONDON • MELBOURNE • VANCOUVER

Broken & Redeemed

Finding Freedom through Complete Surrender

Published in New York, New York, by Morgan James Publishing. Morgan James is a trademark of Morgan James, LLC. www.MorganJamesPublishing.com

Proudly distributed by Ingram Publisher Services.

Author website: www.brokenandredeemed.com

Morgan James BOGO™

A **FREE** ebook edition is available for you or a friend with the purchase of this print book.

[   ]

CLEARLY SIGN YOUR NAME ABOVE

Instructions to claim your free ebook edition:
1. Visit MorganJamesBOGO.com
2. Sign your name CLEARLY in the space above
3. Complete the form and submit a photo of this entire page
4. You or your friend can download the ebook to your preferred device

ISBN 9781631958298 paperback
ISBN 9781631958304 ebook
Library of Congress Control Number:
2021950248

Cover Design by:
Rachel Lopez
www.r2cdesign.com

Interior Design by:
Christopher Kirk
www.GFSstudio.com

Editorial:
Inspira Literary Solutions
Gig Harbor, WA

Morgan James is a proud partner of Habitat for Humanity Peninsula and Greater Williamsburg. Partners in building since 2006.

Get involved today! Visit MorganJamesPublishing.com/giving-back

You have to seek God alone,
but when He meets you, it will be by yourself.
~ A.W Tozer

THE PATH

As I started this journey, I did not know where I was going
Or where I would end up. Only One knew
Only One . . . and He knew from the beginning
Just exactly where I was going and where I would end up.

The path was at times straight, at times rough, winding
And at times ending nowhere—
Thus, forcing me back to where I started.

This path led me to the edge of a cliff.
It was cold and dark, and I stood there, pondering what was next.
Who knows how long I stood
With no direction, no hope, no guidance, no love?

Then the darkness from the storm swept me off the edge.
As I lost my breath, I fell to what looked like the end . . .
Only to land in the arms of the Father.

As I fell into His arms
I heard His voice say,
"I've been waiting for you; welcome home, My son."

It is here where I found direction, hope, guidance, and love.
I was free from my struggles and my past.
I was forgiven from the cross.
I would be emptied, and humbled.
Over time, what I knew as my life would die.

I was then filled with a Spirit
Who would guide me, teach me, forgive me,
And never leave me.

He never said that my path would now be smooth.
In fact, He said that, because of Him, I would face trials and persecution
For His glory.

But I wasn't to fear, as I had in the past
For when this happened, His words would be what I spoke.

I would fall from time to time
But He would be there to catch me
Just as He did on my darkest day.
Trials would come and winds would blow
But through the storms, He would never let me go.

So, as I grow and learn His ways
His love will show me the way.
For now, I obey, and live His way.

~ John Jarman

TABLE OF CONTENTS

Acknowledgments

First and foremost, I want to thank my Lord Jesus Christ, and our God, the Father. I also want to thank:

Adel Jarman (MamaDel), who is with the Lord, for your continuous prayers over my life. It was your prayers that kept me safe over the years until I finally accepted Christ as my Lord and Savior.

Christina Holland, for guidance, wisdom, teaching, support, faith, and the encouragement to write this book. I could not and would not have been able to do this without you. Your commitment to your profession is truly exceptional. God truly blessed me by placing you in my life. The work we did will forever impact my life and my faith. I am finally free from my past!

Scotty Kessler, for your theology, education, wisdom, and guidance in leading me to freedom. I thank God daily for placing you and Life Center in my life. You taught and guided me through my spiritual war. Thank you for teaching me how to do the same for others. I feel blessed to be part of God's team. I could have never written this book without stepping on the battlefield with you. Thank you, my dear brother.

Lynn Matheny Jarman, for all you did for me during our time together. I am truly sorry for the pain and sadness I caused you. I hope one day you can find it in your heart to forgive me. I pray for you every day that your life will have the Lord's blessings.

Leah Noland, for being the strong Christian woman you are and for believing in me, having faith in me, and accepting me for who I am. I thank God for you. My love for you will always be through Christ Jesus, and I pray daily for peace and happiness in your life, and that God blesses you.

Bart Millard, for your time backstage in Kent, Washington. It was an honor meeting you. Your music is a true inspiration for the world. Thank you and MercyMe for permission to use "Dear Younger Me" and other references to this song in this book. I hope you enjoy reading the copy you now have. Until we meet again, may God bless you.

A.J. Swoboda, for your teaching and wisdom, especially in the following books: *Messy, A Glorious Dark: Finding Hope in the Tension Between Belief and Experience, The Dusty Ones: Why Wandering Deepens Your Faith, Subversive Sabbath: Redeeming How We Talk,* and *After Doubt: How to Question Your Faith without Losing It.* Your writing is a true gift, and it has helped me deepen my faith. It was an honor to meet you; I thank you for your time. I hope one day we can meet for coffee.

Duston (DUSTY) Jensen, for believing in me and not only becoming my business partner, but also one of my best friends in life. You, sir, are a true friend. I owe you so much; you have been a blessing in my life. Your wisdom and faith in Summit Strength

& Conditioning were second to none. You took a chance, and even though we had some struggles, we never gave up and never let our friendship weaken. I thank you from the bottom of my heart. It was a great seven-year run.

Denette Colbo, for your belief in my dream. You have made it easier to make this dream come true. I thank the Lord for placing you in my life, and I cherish our friendship. You will remain in my prayers forever. May the Lord bless you and keep you.

Diana Rea Ringer, I cherish our friendship! Without you I would have never started writing again, even though you would from time to time give me a gentle push to start. Now is the time. I think of those texts as I complete this book. Thank you for your friendship, and may our Lord bless you and keep you safe.

Marilyn Tuohy, for your edits on the earliest versions of the book. Your time and commitment are truly appreciated. I hope you are now relaxing and reading our work.

Anna, for your friendship, support, and help over the years as we built Summit. We have been through a lot and our friendship stood strong through it all. In life we find very few true friends; you are one.

The staff at Life Center in Tacoma, Washington, for all your help and support in my walk. You are all a true blessing to me.

Eric Boles, Tyler Sollie, and Eric Tinglum, for all your counseling, prayer, and guidance over the years. Eric, thank you for baptizing me into my new life.

Brandon Stanley and Ryan Jordon, for your friendship and prayers. Brandon, thank you for your willingness to perform at both of my brothers' funeral services.

The numerous athletes and coaches in California, Ohio, North Carolina, Georgia, and Washington who have been a part of my life throughout my coaching career.

Pastors Dr. James MacDonald, Tony Evans, and Rick Warren, although we don't know each other at this time. Your teachings have helped me grow and develop a deep, loving relationship with our Lord and Savior. Reading and listening to your teaching has helped me more than words can express.

Arlyn Lawrence and the staff at Inspira Literary Solutions for all the help and hard work in the editing of *Broken and Redeemed*. Their guidance and Spirit-led suggestions helped shape my story. They had their work cut out for them due to my dyslexia! I truly thank them for making me look so good.

And, finally, Morgan James Publishing for the humbling honor of accepting me into their family of authors. The team outdid themselves on the design of *Broken and Redeemed*. A special shout out to Rachel for her work on the cover.

FOREWORD

When John Jarman enters a room, you can feel his energy. He is strong, aware, and noticeable. There is something palpable about being with him. He is engaging and bright while also being serious and armored-up. I was honored to come to know all of these parts of John.

We met in 2010 during a strange time in his life and I was curious and willing to meet him on his journey. I am a Marriage and Family Therapist, which means I focus on relationships and family dynamics to understand problems and find better perspectives and solutions. Our initial meetings were very thorough family histories and significant milestone stories about his life. But we were both struck by the very large gap in his memories spanning from early childhood to age eleven. We spent many sessions attempting to piece together photographs and oral histories from other family members to create a timeline.

What started as a straightforward family history with childhood trauma morphed into a moment I sometimes wish I could forget. To dismiss it as "transference or projection or hyper awareness" feels false. It was a very cold presence that I never wanted in my space again. But my ethics, training, and moral compass all knew this man needed help with whatever this was. And so we committed to the course of treatment and continued unpacking all of the questions and potential answers. John's relentless attention to detailed research was why I suggested he write a book about his life. I was, and still am, so impressed with this man.

During our work, John challenged me to push myself as a clinician. I met monthly with my Mentor to find more ways to help him. I attended trainings and read texts on spirituality and trauma and found deep reservoirs of information for both of us. I grew in knowledge and experience while walking this path with John. As much as he gained in therapeutic insights or interventions, I gained tenfold by expanding my consciousness to see other concepts not necessarily taught in advanced education programs. For this, I humbly thank you, sir, for your energy and sharing it with me.

Peace be with you.

Christina Holland, LMFT
November 2021

PREFACE

Christina Holland said to me in one of our counseling sessions that I should write a book. Well, Christina, here it is. Seven years later, I've finished the book; thank you for planting the seed.

It took a couple of years for me to begin writing, and six years to complete it. My resistance was twofold: first, I didn't believe my story was worth telling or that anyone would read it. Secondly, I didn't think I was strong enough in my faith to begin the work, let alone complete it. I wouldn't completely give in to God's plan. I questioned everything, and the Spirit continued to work in me. So, I started writing and looking for a ghostwriter, which I never found. After working on the book for about two years, I stopped and put it on the shelf, on hold.

It wasn't until I found myself in the middle of what my friend and mentor, Pastor Eric Boles, called "the perfect storm," followed by four months of daily prayer, that the Holy Spirit led me to pick up my manuscript again and finish writing my story. Then, the writing stopped again when I enrolled in seminary in pursuit of a Master of Theology degree and the knowledge I felt I needed (more on that later). I did this after much counseling with my spiritual mentor and brother, Scotty Kessler.

I was asked numerous times if I was going to become a pastor. I always answered that question the same way: I do not know what God has planned for me, but I am doing this for knowledge so I can have a better understanding of Jesus, God the Father, and the Bible. If the Lord's plan is that I preach the gospel, then that is what I will do. It is in His hands.

I was fifty years old when I truly started learning who God is and what some of His plan is for me. The title of this book, *Broken and Redeemed*, came to me one day during my prayer and study time, so I know it came from the Holy Spirit. We are all broken, but the good news is that when we are ready to come home, we are redeemed. God is waiting for you, just as He waited for me. This is what this book is about. I hope that as you read my story, you will see that the broken, poor, and meek are the ones Jesus came to be with. I read that "God made us without our permission but will not save us without our consent; we have to be open to being healed and saved."[1] This is a spot-on statement. And that is my story.

Jesus told the story of the prodigal son to show us that no matter what we do or how lost we become, the Father is waiting, and He rejoices when we return home. We are all broken in many ways. Each of us may feel we are the only one who has ever gone through what we are going through, but the truth is, we aren't. Many have stood where you are standing, walked the

---

1   Swoboda, A. J. *After Doubt: How to Question Your Faith without Losing It.* Brazos Press, a division of Baker Publishing Group, 2021.

road you're walking. The good news is that we are all redeemed because Jesus went to the cross for us. He redeemed us on the cross and restored our relationship with God.

My knowledge now comes from many areas: the Bible, Faith Seminary, Scotty's teachings, Christina's counseling, church, numerous books, and many Christian artists such as MercyMe, TobyMac, Jeremy Camp, For King & Country, Micha Taylor, and others. I will touch on these more throughout the book. I am not a pastor, or a theologian, or a history professor, or a Bible professor. I am just a flawed, broken human who knew nothing of Christ, the Church, or the Bible until my young adult years. The only mention of God growing up was by my grandmother (MamaDel), when I visited her in Arkansas. She would always tell me, "Johnny, God has a special plan for you." I think MamaDel was right, and part of that plan, I believe, is the book you are holding in your hands.

In this book, I will tell the story of how I came to know Christ, the mistakes I made along the way, and the things I have learned (and continue to learn) through the messy but glorious walk with Jesus. One of my favorite Christian authors, A.J. Swoboda (whom you'll see quoted often in this book), said, "Christianity is surprisingly messier than what I signed up for."[2] I agree!

I will share with you the redemption that Christ has for us through what He did on the cross for you and me. I will make every effort not to make this about me, but about Him. This is really His story—He is in control; it took me years to understand that.

---

2   Swoboda, A. J. *Messy: God Likes It That Way*. Grand Rapids, MI: Kregel Publications, 2012.

I once heard a pastor say, "You can't have a conversion without a conversion story." My hope is that my story will help just one person understand that no matter what you have been through, or what you might have done, or how long it takes you to come home to Christ, the Holy Spirit is always with you, even when you don't know it or want it. TobyMac has a song called "Scars (Come with Livin')" and I think all of us can attest to that. The good news is that scars came for our redemption; maybe Jesus was trying to teach us something on that dark day. No matter our scars or the pain that we have gone through, are going through, or are about to go through, we are redeemed by His scars.

I'll never forget when I read the following: "It does mean that he knows if this book will sell, yet he won't tell me ahead of time when I want to know. Someone still needs to write it."[3] The very next day for the *My Daily Bread* post, in the "promise" series, came Hebrews 10:36, "Patient endurance is what you need now, so that you will continue to do God's will. Then you will receive all that he has promised" (NLT). I knew right then what the Spirit was telling me. I knew I had to pull out this partially written manuscript again and sit down at the computer and get it finished.

I need you to understand I am not proud of some of the stories you are going to read. But I am proud of the man I have become with God's help. There were times in my life when I thought I was a man of God, but I was fooling myself. More accurately, I was what Pastor Andrew Toeaina calls a "Submarine Christian." I surfaced on Sunday and then went underwater during the week. This was my Christian walk for years. But in

---

3   Ibid.

November of 2016, I truly gave my life completely to our Lord Jesus and started trying to walk the walk. I started reading, listening to, and truly understanding the Word of God. Romans 7:14-21 helped me see the roller coaster I was on and why I did the things I did:

"So, the trouble is not with the law, for it is spiritual and good. The trouble is with me, for I am all too human, a slave to sin. I don't really understand myself, for I want to do what is right, but I don't do it. Instead, I do what I hate. But if I know that what I am doing is wrong, this shows that I agree that the law is good. So, I am not the one doing wrong; it is sin living in me that does it. And I know that nothing good lives in me, that is, in my sinful nature. I want to do what is right, but I can't. I want to do what is good, but I don't. I don't want to do what is wrong, but I do it anyway. But if I do what I don't want to do, I am not really the one doing wrong; it is sin living in me that does it. I have discovered this principle of life—that when I want to do what is right, I inevitably do what is wrong." (NLT)

I did not get this scripture at first. I had to meditate on it for a while; then it hit me. As Christians, we understand the law and we want to do what is right, but we don't always do it because of our sinful nature. Please don't get me wrong; this does not excuse us from our sin, nor does it justify our sin. It did help me to understand that, even as a Christian, I still have sin. It just doesn't go away when we come to Christ, and we all must be aware of this.

My transgressions are many and I am working toward purification through the Lord. I take full responsibility for my actions and have asked for forgiveness from those whom I have hurt. We all fall, but what do we do when we fall? Do we stay in the darkness? We will stumble from time to time, even when we find true relationship with Christ. Following Jesus is not about being perfect; none of us are perfect. It's about repentance.

God's Word says we find salvation and sanctification through Christ Jesus. Working through my sins and confronting my mistakes has been painful, but I'm finding freedom. My hope and prayers are that this book gives someone else the same freedom I now have in the Lord. I am not writing this for you to feel sorry for me; I see this book as part of my repentance and healing. I have heartfelt sorrow for those touched by my sin. The changes in my behavior and thinking have been the work of God. James McDonald captures this change perfectly: "The growth I have seen has been in three areas: first, the length of time between failures has become much longer, second, the amount of time it takes to see my fault and apologize has become shorter, and third, my awareness of when I might be tempted so I can avoid the situation altogether has become acute. Less failure, less severe, fewer excuses, but still not perfect."[4]

For the protection of the people in my story, and the respect and consideration of others, some names have been changed and selected people and details have been omitted from this account. My intent is to tell the story God has given me to tell, without hurting anyone or causing more pain from my sins.

Thank you for reading my story. My prayer is that it touches your heart in some way and you take something from these pages

---

4   McDonald, *Act Like A Man: 40 Days to Biblical Manhood*, 2014

that you can use in your life. May you find the peace in Christ as I have, and may God truly bless you.

I have placed questions at the end of each chapter to help you look into your relationship with God. These questions will challenge you and hopefully deepen your faith. They will help you examine yourself and your walk. They don't need to be completed as you read this book. You can come back and answer them later, or, if you choose, you can get a group together and read a chapter a week and then discuss your answers with one another. If you choose this option make sure that you are with a trusted group, and that you all agree that what is said in your study stays in that study room.

My goal with this book is to simply share what God has done for me, and how my life and faith have changed since I started my walk with Him. If you are already a Christian, I hope this helps your faith increase. If you are not a follower of Jesus, and you return home to the Father, that would be the biggest blessing. Whatever your situation, I hope you enjoy this book no matter where you are in your walk with Him.

~ John Jarman

Chapter One

Redemption

"Once we, too, were foolish and disobedient. We were misled and became a slave to many lusts and pleasures. Our lives were full of evil and envy, and we hated each other. But—when God our Savior relived his kindness and love, he saved us, not because of the righteous thing we had done, but because of his mercy. He washed away our sins, giving us a new birth and new life through the Holy Spirit. He generously poured out his Spirit upon us through Jesus Christ our Savior. Because of his grace he made us right in his sight and gave us confidence that we will inherit eternal life." (Titus 3:3-7, NIV)

In November of 2016, I encountered the biggest storm I've ever experienced. I had become a believer in Jesus and was moving closer to God in my daily prayer and reading time. Then the trials came pouring in.

My business was struggling so badly I thought I would lose everything. My sister-in-law re-entered the hospital, battling liver and kidney failure, and eventually passed away. My girl-friend of four years broke up with me. Having this relationship end after trying so hard to "do everything right," a relationship committed to God at the center of our lives, was both unexpected and difficult.

As I went through this stormy season, a particular Bible passage came to mind often:

> *"So, if you think you are standing firm, be careful that you don't fall! No temptation has overtaken you except what is common to mankind. And God is faithful; he will not let you be tempted beyond what you can bear. But when you are tempted, he will also provide a way out so that you can endure it." (1 Corinthians 10:12-13, NIV)*

I would reflect often on this passage. I thought, *God must think I have really big shoulders because I am bearing a lot.*

Giving It All to God

Then, one day, I heard pastor Tony Evans present a different perspective on this verse. He started by saying he was going to share with us the only verse in the Bible that is not true: 1 Corinthians 10:12-13. He continued with saying, "If God gives us what we can handle, we don't need Him. So, He is going to give us more than we can handle so there is only one way to look: and that is up."

And that is what God did. In the wee hours of the morning of November 22, 2016, I was broken to the point that I didn't know what to do or where to turn, and I needed help. I had only one way to look, and that was up.

At 3:30 a.m., falling to my knees, I prayed to God in a way I had never prayed before. I cried out loud to Him all my fear, hurt, desperation, and confusion. I told God everything that was in my heart. With tears running down my face, I opened my Bible and just started flipping pages and reading passages. One of the first that caught my attention was 1 John 1:5-10:

> *"This is the message we have heard from him and declares to you: God is light, in him there is no darkness at all. If we claim to have fellowship with him and yet walk in darkness, we lie and do not live out the truth. But if we walk in the light, as he is in the light, we have fellowship with one another, and the blood of Jesus, his Son, purifies us from all sin. If we claim to be without sin, we deceive ourselves and the truth is not in us. If we confess our sins, he is faithful and just and will forgive us our sins and purify us from all unrighteousness. If we claim we have not sinned, we make him out to be a liar and his word is not in us." (1 John 1:5-10, NIV)*

As soon as I read this, I knew this is what I had been doing, and that this was the reason I was on my knees. Well-known Christian author A.W. Tozer said it well: "The sinner prides himself on his independence, completely overlooking the fact that he is a weak slave of the sins that rule his members. The man who surrenders to Christ exchanges a cruel slave driver for a kind and gentle Master whose yoke is easy and whose burden is light."[5]

---

5   Tozer, A. W. *The Pursuit of God: The Human Thirst for the Divine*. Chicago: Moody Publishers, 2015.

Some people think God punishes His children. I know now that God disciplines His children just like our earthly fathers do. As I thought about this question over a few days, I thought I would go to the Bible to see if I could find a way to clear this up for all of us. I found sixty-four verses that speak to discipline and, of those, forty-seven are in the Old Testament and seventeen are in the New Testament. I have included a few of these here:

> *I will be his father and he will be my son. If he sins, I will correct him and discipline him with a rod, like any father would do."* (2 Samuel 7:14, NLT)

> *"But consider the joy of those corrected by God! Don't despise the discipline of the Almighty when you sin."* (Job 5:17, NLT)

> *"Yet when we are judged by the Lord, we are being disciplined so that we will not be condemned along with the world."* (1 Corinthians 11:32, NLT)

> *"If God doesn't discipline you as he does all of his children, it means that you are illegitimate and are not really his children at all."* (Hebrews 12:8, NLT)

Looking back on that season and that pivotal night, I believe God wanted me to move to the next level in our relationship and His plan for me, but I needed to be right with Him in order to do that. So, this was His wake-up call. I had to be shown that I needed to give everything, just as He asked His disciples to do.

I had been following Jesus in some ways, but there were still things I had been unwilling to give up or change. Control was the biggest of these. Having been in control of my life for so long, doing things my way had become the way I lived.

This wasn't the only thing keeping me from true fellowship with Jesus. I had two other major strongholds in my life with which I still struggle daily: anger (or what some of my friends call my "bark") and lust. The latter is one of the biggest strongholds that keeps men from finding true fellowship with Jesus. Dr. James MacDonald said that lust is the number one stronghold with which men at his men's conferences admit they struggle. **Men, I am telling you right now, give it to God.** Confess your sin and humble yourself at the foot of the cross. Admit your weakness and God will change you. It may take some time, but with your focus and His help, He will renew your mind and you will be set free.

The next passage that stood out to me on that November early morning was 2 Corinthians 1:8-10. After reading and thinking about these verses, I decided to personalize them, like this:

"We do not want you to be uninformed, brothers and sisters, about the troubles I experienced in the town of Tacoma, Washington. I was under great pressure, far beyond my ability to endure, so that I despaired of life itself. Indeed, I felt I had received the sentence of death. But this happened that I might not rely on myself but on God, who raises the dead. He has delivered me from such a deadly peril, and he will deliver me again. On him I have set my hope that he will continue to deliver me." (paraphrase mine)

If you look up this verse in your own Bible, you'll see how I changed a few words to make its message personal to me. This is an exercise I do quite often now. When the Word speaks to my heart while I am reading it, I simply insert myself into the text.

These verses changed my faith and devotion to Christ. I gave up control that morning and I haven't looked back. I started journaling. Previously, whenever I heard pastors or others advocate journaling, I would respond that I didn't have time, didn't want to do it, and didn't see how it would help. Yet, once I began, the benefits were immediate and obvious. Now, many months later, I see how the Holy Spirit has used this simple tool to probe, stretch, and deepen my faith and my relationship with God.

Growing Spiritually

I needed something else to help me stay focused. I needed the fellowship and community the Bible tells us we need. I was attending church, but I needed more, so I looked for a small group Bible study. After exploring some options, I joined a Bible Study Fellowship group I had heard about from a friend. The first week I attended, they were reading through the book of John, and I was coming in at chapter nine. I had some time to kill before the meeting, so I sat in a local Applebee's restaurant, reviewing the lesson, and asking the Holy Spirit to show me why I was going through this storm. As I turned the page of my Bible back to the start of John 9, two verses jumped off the page:

His disciples asked him, "Rabbi, who sinned, this man or his parents, that he was born blind?" "Neither this man nor his parents sinned," said Jesus, "but this happened so that the works of God might be displayed in him." (John 9:2-3, NIV)

As soon as I read this, I thought, *This is why I have been going through this storm. I was going through this storm not because of my sins, but so the power and glory of God could be seen through me.* A peace came over me like I have never known. I said, "Okay, God. If this is Your will, then I accept it and I trust that You will get me through this for Your glory. Whatever You want me to do, I will do. Whatever I need to go through, I will go through." I knew that no matter what was ahead of me, God would protect me and bring me through it so I could give Him all the glory and honor.

Now, as you read this, if you are a non-believer, you are most likely calling me crazy. If you are a believer, you understand what I was feeling. It's been six years since then and I can say that the Lord has been good to me. It has not been all smooth; there have been ups and downs. Christianity is not always a bed of roses. Faith makes it more doable. We learn how to praise Jesus in the storm. It's easy to praise the Lord when things are going well, but can you praise Him in the storm? As our faith deepens, it shows us how we can and must praise Him in the storm as well.

I have told people from time to time that, next to Paul, I am likely the world's second biggest sinner. By the grace of God, Paul was saved. Jesus said, "Healthy people don't need a doctor—

sick people do. I have come to call not those who think they are righteous, but those who know they are sinners and need to repent" (Luke 5:31, NLT). And if God saved Paul, He could save you and me.

In Paul's first letter to Timothy, he wrote, "But for that very reason I was shown mercy so that in me, the worst of sinners,

Christ Jesus might display his immense patience as an example for those who would believe in him and receive eternal life" (1 Timothy 1:16, NIV) We are saved by grace; this is God's gift! I now know that in Him I am loved, redeemed, forgiven, and free.

As I prayed that night, I looked back on my life and its pattern of constant struggle. I had been walking in darkness even though I had seen the light of Jesus. In his book, *Redeeming How We Talk*, A.J. Swoboda shares this story:

"A young man we know tells a story. He has dreams and desires—many of which are in his reach—to become an artist. Yet, every time he gets close to living these dreams, he makes some decision that ultimately undermines what he wants to do. He keeps pulling the rug out from under his own feet."[6]

This was my life up to this point: I would get close to my dream, only to pull the rug from under my own feet. I wasn't doing my part in my relationship with God. The storm I was experiencing was God's way of showing me this and preparing me for my destiny.

This was the beginning of my true salvation and sanctification. I say "beginning," because sanctification is continuous as we grow in Christ. In his book, *Act Like Men: 40 Days to Biblical Manhood*, James MacDonald writes, "Salvation launches for you personally at the moment of your repentance and faith. Salvation then continues through life as God sanctifies you bit by bit, conforming you to the likeness of His Son." I believe that

---

6 Wytsma, Ken, and A. J. Swoboda. *Redeeming How We Talk: Discover How Communication Fuels Our Growth, Shapes Our Relationships, and Changes Our Lives.* Chicago: Moody Publishers, 2018.

even when I was not walking "in the light," God was still working on my sanctification and watching over me.

With that, I think it's time to tell you my story. But first, I ask you to take a few minutes to think with your heart and answer a few questions. Be honest and let the Spirit guide you. If you want to receive the most benefit, I recommend discussing your answers with a trusted friend or writing them in a journal. Even if you're not ready to do either of these, I hope you'll at least pause for a moment to think about these few questions. They've impacted my own life immeasurably; I believe they can change yours as well.

REFLECTION or DISCUSSION

What is the biggest obstacle blocking your relationship with Christ?

Read Romans 7:14-25 and describe how it applies to you. What do you know you shouldn't do, but do anyway?

Read 1 John 1:5-8 and describe how it applies to you now or has applied to your past.

Chapter Two

MY EARLY YEARS

"We can rejoice, too, when we run into problems and trials, for we know that they help us develop endurance. And endurance develops strength of character, and character strengthens our confident hope of salvation. And this hope will not lead to disappointment. For we know how dearly God loves us, because he has given us the Holy Spirit to fill our hearts with his love." (Romans 5:3-5, NLT)

I was born on January 15, 1964, in Little Rock, Arkansas, to Jerry and Donna (Dodge) Jarman. My dad came from a Southern Methodist family that included Harry Chub ("Papa Chub" to me), Adel (MamaDel), and his sister Jean. Both Jean and Dad were adopted. My mom came from a much larger family, comprised of Eddie (Grandpa), Martha (Grandma), three blood brothers (Chuck, Denny, and Tommy), two adopted brothers (Jack and Michael), and one adopted sister (Jill).

Dad grew up in Arkansas; Mom hailed from upstate New York. The two met while Dad was in the Air Force, and were married on July 4, 1959, in a Catholic Church just down the street from my maternal grandparents' home in San Pedro, New Mexico. I was the third born of four boys: Steve, Jerry II (David), me, and Jason. I learned from family stories that we lived in Fort Smith, Arkansas until I was four years old, and then relocated to the Pacific Northwest. We moved around south King County more times than I can remember, mostly living in Des Moines and Renton as my brothers and I grew up.

Eight months after I was born, I would be in a battle for my life. I don't know the cause of what happened, but from the stories that my family shared, I know some of the details of the events that took place. I was taken to the hospital with what was to be diagnosed as Osteomyelitis in my upper left arm. I do not know what this was or what caused this; it was only after researching Osteomyelitis and talking with a few orthopedic doctors that I found out its cause is from staphylococcus bacteria. From my research, I understand there are only two ways that one can contract this: 1) from an open fracture, or 2) a severe case of pneumonia. My upper left arm still bears three scars from this.

The thing I don't understand is that I don't have any pictures from this time in my life, nor can I seem to locate any. We lost my dad in '03 and my mom in '08, so the only people who might have known what happened are a couple of my uncles and my oldest brother. I talked to my uncles, and they didn't know about the surgeries.

After hearing this, I wish I would have started looking into what happened before my parents, grandparents, and others passed away. I look back now and sometimes wonder, *Why didn't I find out what really caused this to happen? What procedures were used? What did the doctor's notes say, if they could be found?*

This curiosity about what happened grew as I was in counseling. Even as I went through college and became more educated about the human body, I didn't think to look into it. But through counseling, I began looking at my life. I wanted the answer to the question of what had happened to my arm. Was I told the truth? So, I started the search. I contacted the hospitals that were open in 1964; two of them told me they had no record of me being in that hospital. The other told me the warehouse that stored their microfilm had caught fire and they'd lost half of their records. So, I was left to wonder.

According to my mom, after the second surgery, the doctor entered the waiting room. He stood silently without saying anything. She asked him if I was okay, and he said nothing. Then apparently, I started crying from somewhere in the direction from which the doctor had come, and he told my mother to listen. He confirmed that I was the one crying and I had made it through the second of two surgeries. When I finally left the hospital, I was eight months old with my left arm in a half-cast. This is the only account of these scars I have.

As I said, I found no pictures of me at this age, nor can I seem to locate any within my family. My uncles told me they didn't know about the surgery when it occurred. When they later saw the scars, they apparently believed the same story I had been told. My brother David doesn't recall much because he was just three years old when I had the surgery. Neither does Steve, my other older brother, remember any significant information. So, the wondering continued.

Three months after the arm surgeries, I was apparently back in the hospital fighting a severe case of pneumonia. My mom told me I went into convulsions while at home and a neighbor prevented me from swallowing my tongue by holding it until the EMTs arrived at the house. I spent another month in the hospital. This story was corroborated by Steve.

I also learned from Steve that Mom left Dad shortly after I recovered from these two medical events—the surgery and the seizure. Steve is unable to recall everything about that time, but he does remember being on a train with Mom, Dave, and me. He thinks we were in Chicago when Dad caught up to us. I find this odd because Mom's family was in New Mexico at the time. But I suppose if she was running, she was trying to hide. Steve's memories line up with Jason's and Uncle Denny's accounts of Mom and Dad being married to one another twice, or perhaps just separated, as I only found one marriage certificate in my research.

Missing Memories

I have no memory of my childhood until I was around age twelve or thirteen. In fact, it is weird to try to reflect on my earliest years. I can look at pictures of people I was with and events where I was present, and not recall any of it at all. I know we didn't spend a lot of "family time" together, such as family dinners and trips. And I have known for a while that abuse and other troubling events happened within our family which is what put me into counseling for ten-plus years and led me to serve as a volunteer for the Pierce County Chapter of NAMI (National Alliance of Mental Illness). I will be touching on this later in the book.

I heard stories about alleged abuse that took place in my family. When I heard this, I thought there was no way it had happened to me, not realizing that I didn't really recall my childhood at that time. For years, I held on to this belief that I was not a victim. I really didn't question my childhood until years into counseling. It was not until I was working with Christina, and we were in about the fifth year of counseling, when I started having thoughts that maybe, just maybe, I didn't escape the abuse. What I came to realize was that I had actually been right in the middle of it.

I spent months researching my family history and talking to family members to find out as much information as I could about my life as an infant, toddler, child, and pre-teen. The accounts I collected represent the only picture I have of these years. Almost everything I "know" about my life before age twelve, I know from stories told to me by others, not experiences I remember or facts I have been able to verify. I never had any reason to doubt them, and perhaps everything I was told is indeed true. But significant gaps in the narrative, and information about the past that I was able to put together, have left me with questions—questions to which only God knows the answers.

When I first understood there was a possibility that I had been physically abused, I wanted to know what had happened, no matter how dark it was. But one day changed that. I was in a session with Christina, and we were working on finding the answer to this question. Though some may not believe or accept what I will share later about this, both Christina and I can recall the happenings of that day like it was yesterday

I knew of God while growing up, but that was about it. We didn't go to church. I don't think I prayed at all during my childhood unless I thought I was in trouble. (Maybe you know what I'm talking about: those prayers said when you are in a tight spot— "God, please get me through and I promise I won't do this again and I will do anything You ask"—after which you keep on doing what you were doing without changing anything in your life.

Fast forward to age five. I was back in the hospital for twenty stitches in the middle of my forehead, leaving another scar that is still visible today. According to what I have been told, the injury was the result of me running to the car, tripping, and hitting my head on the bottom of the open-door frame. Apparently, the stitches were applied with just a local anesthetic; my mom told me they had to hold me down for the procedure.

One childhood experience I do remember was an occasion when I was riding bikes with my friends. Like most kids at that time, we were building ramps and jumping our bikes or racing them or just getting crazy. On that day, I hit the ramp, took off, made the landing, but ran out of room and couldn't stop in time. Bam, I ran right into a fence, splitting my head open again just above my right eye.

What I do recall is that life was hard from the start. It was a fight, and as a child, I was up against threats that were much bigger and stronger than me. While God protected me on many levels, it's clear today that I sustained wounds during that season of my life—some visible, some invisible.

With Christina's guidance, I began looking at my life, and at the allegations of abuse within my family of which I could have been a victim. Suddenly, I had a pile of questions with no ready answers. *Had I been told the truth? If I had, why did so few people know about my surgeries, and why had I never been told what led to it?*

Generational Sin?

Looking back now, I believe my family most likely has been impacted by generational sin, some of which still has some influence over me and other family members. What is "generational sin?" The Old Testament talks about it in Deuteronomy 5:9-10:

"You shall not bow down to them or worship them; for I, the Lord your God, am a jealous God, punishing the children for the sin of the parents to the third and fourth generation of those who hate me, but showing love to a thousand generations of those who love me and keep my commandments."

I didn't understand this verse until about three years ago. Now that I know generational sin is real, I can see some indication of its presence in my family history. The unknown identity of my dad's parents leaves many questions unanswered regarding my paternal lineage.

Meanwhile, what I have learned about my (Dodge) grandfather's past strongly indicates some generational sin within my maternal genealogy that not only affected me but my brothers and other family members as well. I think this is something we each need to consider when we ask for forgiveness when we come to the Lord. If we know about this kind of thing in our family, then we must pray for the forgiveness of these sins as well. Generational sin can place spiritual strongholds on us— patterns of ongoing sin and bondage—and these are tough to break. It takes time and prayer with someone who understands this dynamic and knows how to deal with the demonic powers that exist in this world.

My search for the missing pages and chapters of my story continued. However, my work with a counselor and many months of prayer have led me to conclude that perhaps I don't recall my earliest years because I am not supposed to. Whatever happened to me, I made it through by the grace of God. Jesus was watching over me; He cared for me and showed His love for me even though I didn't know Him. I think this is important for us to understand that, when you have people praying over you as I did, the Spirit covers you even in your nightmares or your stupidity. And I think the Holy Spirit continues to protect me by shielding me from even the memories of these events. I believe that this was the first "God Thing" I recognized in my life.

Family Matters

While growing, up my relationships with my brothers were distant at best, with Steve, Dave, and me each doing our own thing and Jason being five years younger. I would say that I was closest to Dave. He and I had more in common; unfortunately, after my dad left, what Dave and I had in common was the parting. We did spend more time together than I did with Steve or Jason.

Steve spent most of his time working and with my mom and our grandparents. Jason would be with them until he was old enough to start doing his own thing. I will tell you this: we loved and supported each other the best we could, and if one needed the other, we would be there in a minute for the other.

Through those years, I didn't have a close relationship with my mom, though she did support me in all of my athletics during high school. We boys didn't see our dad very often. He would come around once in a while, or he would bring us or me over to Colorado where he ended up living out his life with my stepmom.

Our family never had a sit-down family dinner. I cannot recall one time in my life other than at Thanksgiving that we sat together for a meal, and this was always at my grandparents' place. There were good years and bad years, and our relationships all morphed in various ways over time. But we stayed together as best we could.

My MamaDel was a strong Southern Baptist. Even though I didn't spend a lot of time with her, she played a big part in my life and my walk with God, once I accepted Christ. God was working through her for decades to get me to invite Jesus into my life, but I wanted no part of it. I was into me. It took over fifty years for me to truly say yes to Jesus and fully surrender. And for the years of my life that MamaDel was here, I believe that she prayed daily for our salvation.

She used to tell me God had a special plan for me because of the challenges I faced—and survived—as a child. During my teen and early adult years, she would say, "Johnny, God has something special planned for you."

I always shrugged it off. "Yeah, right, Grandma." I didn't believe her.

But she believed what she said and repeated it to me every chance she got. Now, here I am, writing my story, and I know MamaDel has a big smile on her face in heaven. I should have known she was right.

When MamaDel passed away, Lynn (my wife at the time) and I went to Arkansas to help my dad with the memorial service. I was grateful to be able to keep two of her possessions that are very special to me. One is her Bible. Going through it and reading her notes has been a priceless gift. The other item of hers that I treasure is her Holy Trinity cross necklace, which I have worn since her service. She is always with me.

Mama Del's Cross Necklace

Page from Mama Del's Bible

Following the service, our trip back to Ohio held an additional unexpected blessing. I had picked a couple of songs for MamaDel's memorial, one of which was Vince Gill's, "Go Rest High on that Mountain." On our way home, we stopped at the Grand Ole Opry, and while we were there, Vince showed up and played that song—an experience I will always remember.

I miss MamaDel and can hardly wait until we are together again one day in heaven. In the meantime, I imagine her seeing my life now and saying with a smile, "I told you, Johnny. God had something special planned for you. He still does."

I wrote the following for her service, and it was published in the service program:

The lives she touched
over the years and across many miles,
the lives she touched were ones she loved...
and ones of need.
She gave her love without regret;
it was this love
that kept her near
when we needed her the most.

Her spirit remains . . .
so let's not forget:
we all benefitted from her special gift.
Remember one thing:
as we go each day . . .
when we gaze at the sky
with troubled hearts,
the one that will touch us
is always in our hearts.

-John Jarman

Bottom line: God is always with us, and He is waiting for us.
He will even knock at your door from time to time. The question
is, will you open the door and let Him into your heart?

RELFECTION or DISCUSSION
What is your earliest memory from your childhood?

After reading Deuteronomy 5:9-10, and reading my story, do you believe "generational sin" exists? How would you explain it?

Looking back on your early childhood, how would you describe evidence of "generational sin" in your own family? How has it affected you and other family members?

Name a person in your life whom you know or think may have prayed for you. Why do you suppose he or she did this, and how do you believe it has impacted your life?

Chapter Three

SHATTERED

"They will roar like lions, like the strongest of lions. Growling, they will pounce on their victims and carry them off, and no one will be there to rescue them. They will roar over their victims on that day of destruction like the roaring of the sea. If someone looks across the land, only darkness and distress will be seen; even the light will be darkened by clouds." (Isaiah 5:29-30, NLT)

What happened when I was twelve or thirteen changed my family and my life in every possible way. The change was something I would not really understand until years later.

My dad was an alcoholic who became angry and violent when he drank. He would often come home drunk and then destroy items in the house or beat my mother and possibly my brothers and me, although I have no clear memory of this. I know he completely shattered our dining room table set more than once; those were the good nights, because dishes and tables took the abuse rather than people.

One night or early morning, I woke to the sounds of my dad beating my mom—a sound that became all too common. This time, I got up and went down the hall toward the sounds. When I got to where I could see, all I will say is that it is something that no twelve-year-old should see his father doing. Neither of them noticed I was in the kitchen. I moved to a drawer, opened it, pulled out a knife, and shouted, "Stop!"

My dad finally paused and turned toward me. I yelled again, "Stop beating my mom, or I will kill you!" My dad could have taken the knife from me. I am not sure why he didn't. Instead, he stopped and left the house. At that moment, all of our lives changed. It was an irreversible shift for all of us. My dad moved out the next day.

Suffering the Effects of Divorce

Years passed before I saw my father again. Life became very hard for mom, my brothers, and me. Looking back now, I cannot believe that I made it through this and the next decade of my life. There were times when we didn't know where our next meal was coming from. My mom did the best she could and held us together, with Steve's help.

I'm going to take a moment to share some facts on divorce and abuse in families so that maybe it will prevent a child from going through what we did. A note to parents who are divorced, divorcing, or struggling to get along: please, please don't speak badly of each other to your kids. What my mom did—blaming and criticizing my dad to my brothers and me—was so damaging. And research has told us for decades that the effects of divorce on children are profound:

- Teens who experience divorce are four times more likely to use drugs than teens whose parents stay together (which ALL of us ended up doing).
- Sociologists Sara McLanahan and Gary Sandefur found that 31 percent of adolescents with divorced parents dropped out of high school (Steve and Dave both dropped out), compared to 13 percent of children in intact families. They also concluded that 33 percent of adolescent girls whose parents divorced became teen mothers, compared to 11 percent of girls whose parents remained married.[7]
- McLanahan and her colleagues found that 11 percent of boys in divorced families end up spending time in prison before the age of thirty-two (by the grace of God none of us ended up in jail), compared to five percent of boys raised in intact homes.
- Nicholas Wolfinger, demographer, indicates that the adult children of divorce are 89 percent more likely to also divorce (which all but Steve went through; Steve never married).

Author A.J. Swoboda wrote, "The problem with this kind of 'modeling' is that it doesn't model two things' people need to learn how to do: argue and forgive. We are effectively teach-

---

7   McLanahan, S., & Sandefur, G. *Growing Up with a Single Parent: What Hurts, What Helps.* Cambridge, MA: Harvard University Press, 1994.

ing our children how to argue without showing them how to reunite."[8] I want to continue on A.J.'s point, that this type of behavior doesn't model a loving relationship. In any relationship, you are going to have peaks and valleys. If you have unconditional love and honesty in any relationship, you then can get through anything. Jesus modeled this for us when He asked His heavenly Father to take the cross from Him. But, because of the love for His Father, Jesus was able to move through the suffering and be with His Father again.

My oldest brother Steve dropped out of high school; he was in the eleventh grade and got a job to help provide money for food and bills. David also quit school in the tenth grade. I stayed in school, but only as a means for my own non-academic pursuits, which I will tell about in more detail later. All of my brothers and I ended up using and/or abusing both drugs and alcohol. Three of the four of us married and then divorced. Dave and Jason remarried and stayed with their second wives until the passing of Dave and Jessica. I believe that alcohol and drug abuse played a significant role in the death of my dad, Steve, Dave, and Jessica.

I understand the seemingly insurmountable difficulties of marital conflict; divorce is a part of my own story. But if you are a parent, whether you and your spouse are apart or together, I hope my married readers will recognize that the two of you—you and your spouse—are connected for life through your kids, and you need to work together whether you are together or apart to show your children a loving atmosphere. I would hope that

---

8   Swoboda, A. J. *A Glorious Dark: Finding Hope in the Tension between Belief and Experience.* Grand Rapids Baker Books, 2015.

you provide spiritual leadership for them and raise them to be strong men and women of God. I encourage you to seek help and support, not only for yourself, your spouse, and your marriage, but for your kids as well. Talk to a pastor or a counselor and let him or her provide you with guidance. Pray and read the Word so the Holy Spirit can guide you as well. Be actively supportive of your children in every way, including connecting them with mentors and counselors.

Finding My Own Way Out

As I said, all of us used alcohol and drugs growing up. It was the early 80s, and seemingly everyone was doing it. That doesn't make it right; it's just a fact about the times. I was involved in this from about age thirteen to twenty-three. Keg parties, and every drug I could get my hands on, other than heroin. I did these all through school while managing to maintain an above-average athletic career.

This went on for ten years. I remember hosting a party on New Year's Eve 1986, and sitting on my couch and looking around thinking, *There has to be more to life than this.* I got up, left, and never used drugs again. Two days later, I went to the Marine recruiter's office. I walked into the office and said to the Marine sitting there, "I need to get out of here as quick as I can."

He said, "Why, did you commit a crime?"

"Yes," I answered, "but I have not been caught."

He asked, "What did you do?"

I went through everything. I asked how long it would take to get me to boot camp.

He asked, "Why the Marines?"

I answered, "They are the best and the uniforms are badass."

He explained what I had to do before I could go, then finished by saying he could have me in boot camp by the first part of March. My life was about to change forever. I believe this was the Holy Spirit leading me and I didn't even know who that was. As Micah Tyler said in his song "Never Been a Moment":

> *"There's never been a moment*
> *I was not held inside Your arms*
> *And there's never been a day when*
> *You were not who You say You are*
> *You're forever, it don't matter what I'm walking through*
> *'Cause no matter where I'm going*
> *There's never been a moment*
> *That I was not loved by You."*

I see these words as evidence that God is with us even when we do not know Him or want Him. We are still His. As I matured as a Christian, I knew this to be the case. There is no way I would have made it through that time in my life without some divine intervention.

One assignment Christina gave me was to write a letter to my mom and dad, articulating my feelings about my growing up years. I want to share this letter here, just as a way to be transparent about what I worked through in counseling. Counseling, if you let it, can open up the deepest parts of your heart. But you have to want the self-knowledge, or it won't work.

Here is what I was able to express:

Dear Mom and Dad,

I'm writing to you to tell you how much you hurt me through your actions, either known or unknown to yourself. Whether unintentionally or intentionally, the pain, the sadness, and the shame, cost me, due to your actions, or the actions you allowed others to do. Whether it was physical and/or mental abuse, I don't know, because I have blocked that time from any conscious memory. You took my childhood; you took my innocence by these actions. I will say first and foremost that I forgive you, but that doesn't stop the pain, the sadness, or the shame. As a Christian, it is what I'm called to do; however, it will take some time for that to happen. But maybe one day I can truly, truly forgive you.

I want you to know how much this shame has cost me over the years of my life. There are things that have happened to me that I'm responsible for, and some that I'm not responsible for because of all of this. It saddens me telling you, Mom, that when you left this earth, I didn't shed one tear for you. I don't know if I ever miss you.

Whether you knew what you were doing or not (I don't believe you really did), it saddens me. You two are pathetic examples of parents, and you didn't teach me anything about how to be a man, or how to do anything, for that matter. I had to do everything myself. What a shame!

In closing, I will say this: I know now what love is, but it took years to feel that, because I don't even know what love is . . .

Reading this again as I typed it into this book, I had two thoughts: 1) that I might have been a little rough, and 2) that it made me sad. I harbored resentment toward both of my parents for years. I had thought I settled it with them but, after reading this letter, I saw that I still carried it. However, I look at it now and know I am free of that. I can say I love both of them. I understand that they did the best they could and that they, too, were victims. I won't know until I leave this earth if they are in heaven. I hope so, but for now only, God knows.

RELFECTION or DISCUSSION

Describe the toughest situation you faced in your early childhood.

Looking back on your early years, how do you see the Holy Spirit working in your life?

How has your parents' behavior affected your character, positively and/or negatively?

Do you know a child who is facing a shattered time in his or her life? How can you help?

Chapter Four

FATHERLESS

". . . defending the fatherless and the oppressed, so that mere earthly mortals will never again strike terror." (Psalm 10:18, NIV)

This is our Heavenly Father's promise to us who are fatherless. He will defend us and keep us safe from earthly attacks. He did this for me. I spent most of my teen years without a father and during those times I had no idea this Psalm existed. I would say that my development—as far as my identity—was based on the friends I ran around with and a few of the teachers I had in high school. It was not until I was in seminary that I realized I had two fathers. And even though my earthly father was gone during these times, and I hated him for that, my Heavenly Father was watching over and caring for me.

Growing up fatherless is so common now, and I believe that it is one of the biggest issues we face in our society. For me, at the time, I really didn't give it much thought. I just did what I did. Looking back on this time of my life is painful. It saddens me when I reflect, and it's hard not to compare my life to others. I carried shame for years because of the situation that my brothers and I were in. During this time of my life, I never let anyone see what I was going through. My friends never came to my house. I wouldn't talk about home. I was embarrassed by the way we had to live. I felt that if my friends found out, then they wouldn't want to be my friends. I never brought my girlfriend over to my house.

This shame continued into my adult life. There were years that I couldn't and didn't look into the mirror because I didn't like the person looking back at me.

Going Down the Wrong Path

With no real guidance from a parent, I just did what I wanted to. I didn't really put much thought into anything but self-indulgence. I lived day by day, minute by minute; some of you might understand what I am talking about. Looking back on these years, I had a quick temper and got into a lot of fights. I didn't like school and didn't want to go to school. I didn't care about the grades I received; I went mainly for the socialization and to plan parties and sell drugs, and to play football and throw the shot and discus.

I want to say that I am not proud of these stories, and I have asked the Lord and those who were hurt by me in these years for forgiveness. I left out the names of those involved to protect them. I share these stories for one reason: so you can understand where I came from and that, if God can save a sinner like me, He can certainly save you. As Pastor Martin said, "It is how

God chooses the unlikeliest people to accomplish God's desires for the world."[9]

Let me start in the eighth grade. As I said, I had a temper and I got into a lot of trouble—so much so that I had to repeat the eighth grade. I was expelled from school, after I was sent to an alternative school, where I was kicked out the first day for fighting. The next year, as I started school, I found football again. I had played football from the time I was eight to when I started junior high.

So, I started playing football and this was a great release for me. It allowed me to let my frustrations out on the field without getting into trouble. I will say that it did not stop my temper; I held on to this for a long time. I made it through that year and then we moved to Renton. This was where we would stay until I graduated high school and joined the Marines.

Football and track were my thing, along with the weight room, during high school. I have to say that, without them, I would have most likely dropped out of school. We did some crazy things in high school, like taping a friend's brother to the flagpole in the courtyard of the school. We hung another friend's brother from the bridge that went from the gym/student parking lot to the main building. This picture, I believe, made the yearbook. Most likely it would not make it in today; things have changed, and this type of bullying/hazing is not allowed.

My high school had a smoking area for the students. (Yes, you read that correctly. Different times back then.) This is where I hung out during breaks and lunch. I don't know about your school,

---

9   Martin, James. *Jesus: A Pilgrimage*. New York, NY: HarperOne, 2016.

if you are from this era, if you had "cliques," as they called them. We had two distinct groups of students: the jocks and the stoners. I was part of both; because I played football and ran track, I was in the jocks' group. I should not have to tell you why I was part of the other group. I will say this, that there were quite a few students that fell into both of these groups. Some accepted that they belonged to both; others hid the fact from one group to the other.

During high school, there was a party every weekend— "keggers," they called them. These were either at a house or, when weather permitted, in the woods with the location only known to those invited to the party. Some were crazier than others. Some I remember; some I don't. Back then, I drank sometimes so much that I would have blackouts. This is when you wake up the next day and don't remember much of anything from the night before. Thank God I outgrew that. I will save those who attended these parties by not going into details of our times at the keggers. I will say that we did everything you can imagine, and drinking wasn't the only thing going on at these parties—drugs, along with everything else. Enough said.

A Legacy of Coaches

I would like to thank a couple of coaches I had during high school because without them I would have never gone into coaching myself. I truly respected them, and I know that they truly cared about me and wanted the best for me. These are Coach Burkhaulter, Coach Oss, and Coach Newing. All three played a role in keeping me in school and helping develop what little respect for authority I had back then. I had very little, but I learned a lot from the three of them.

As I was writing this chapter, I was in Cairo, Georgia. I was staying with a friend, who is the father of one of my players during my coaching tenure there. We were talking about this topic the morning I was writing this chapter.

Respect—what is it? One definition says this: "a feeling of deep admiration for someone or something elicited by their abilities, qualities, or achievements; due regard for the feelings, wishes, rights, or traditions of others; to admire (someone or something) deeply, as a result of their abilities, qualities, or achievements." This is one element of our society that I feel has been lost.

As Tim and I were talking, I was pointing out that when I was teaching there, all the kids would say "Yes, sir," or, "Yes, ma'am," even if the kid was what teachers called a "problem student." This is commonplace in the South, and it is taught at home, even in fatherless homes. In the Northwest, where I live now, I am not going to say respect isn't taught; it just is not "enforced," for lack of a better term. Having taught in different parts of the country, I can say that respect and discipline is taught less and less in the home. I believe this is a direct result of the fatherless home.

Back to the coaches. Coach Burk was my track coach and strength coach; he also coached football but was not my position coach. Some of the things I do in my strength training still stem from the teachings of Coach Burk. He is the one who planted the seed in me to want to become a coach. During my senior year, he allowed me to coach the freshmen while I did my workouts and he worked with the rest of the throwing team. With his guidance, I was able to have a successful athletic career in high school, placing third in the state at discus throwing. (I still hold the third best discus throw in the history of Lindberg High.) During this time, grades didn't mean much to me, and back then there was no GPA requirement to play sports; all you needed to do was pass the class, even with a D! (Unlike today's student; now an athlete needs a 2.0 GPA to maintain eligibility.)

Coach Newing was our woodshop teacher and head track coach; he saw something in me and took me under his wing in class and gave me a purpose to come to school. He inspired me to start a project that would take the entire year of my junior year. During this year, with his help, I built a handmade steam-bent coat rack, which I still have today. I placed second in the state industrial arts show. I was very proud of that.

Coach Oss was my line coach and, yes, he was hard on us, and he demanded that we do what was right. He pushed us to get the most out of us on the field, and I thank him for that. The three of them—Burk, Oss, and Newing—helped me in preparation for the Corps. I owe these three men a lot. At the time of writing this book, Coach Oss has gone Home to our Father. Coach Burk and Coach Newing, if you are reading this, I thank you for caring about me, teaching me, and most of all inspiring me to be a coach and teacher. It was one of the best choices I have ever made.

If it weren't for these three men, I would have most likely followed my brothers and dropped out of school. Playing sports is what kept me in school. It gave me a sense of belonging. The sad part of this was that my dad never saw me play. Every son wants to make his dad proud, and missing that piece hurt for a long time. My dad did finally make it to one of my athletic events; he came to a game while I was coaching at Ohio U. We were playing Kansas State in Manhattan, Kansas. I can't express how I felt that day. Having him there as I coached healed some of those old wounds.

I truly hope that I was able to help some of the kids that I taught and coached over the years. That is why I got into coaching and teaching. As a teacher/coach, you never know whose life you touched or the impact that you might have had, whether positive or negative. I hate to say it, but in my old life, I know some of the kids didn't feel that I cared for them, and I made a mess with a few of them. It was a tough thing to hear. Humbling myself before them and asking for forgiveness was heartbreaking, but it had to happen, and to receive their forgiveness was a blessing that could only happen through Christ Jesus.

Having gone through this helped me when I worked with some of my students and players who were fatherless during their school years. I was able to share my experiences with them and help them see that they aren't the only ones going through this, and that they could overcome it if they worked for it. I was able to earn the trust of my students and players, so much so that I had a student come to me about her father abusing her.

Some of what we go through in our life isn't our fault and we are, indeed, victims of an injustice. Other times we can make victims of those whom we hurt. One thing I tried to teach my students was that you need to own your mistakes. I didn't always do this; it wasn't until I was in my later years of coaching that I really worked on this. It took years for me to understand the true impact of my transgressions. Owning them was the key to healing and forgiveness. I am currently still working through some of these.

Even though I grew up without a father, God guided my path and looked out for me and those around me. Being fatherless is not the end, but it is definitely a challenge, as you can see. If this is something you are struggling with, I hope that this will give you the courage to keep fighting and know that you can overcome being fatherless. Know that your Father in heaven is with you, no matter what you are going through, and that turning to Him in this storm will make it easier to overcome. Find a mentor, a father figure, who can help you and teach you. Don't let not having a father take you down the wrong path. There are a lot of people who have been without their fathers that have gone on to greatness. Be great and be a great father to your kids, or to whomever God might put into your life who needs a father figure.

RELFECTION or DISCUSSION

What was your biggest hurdle or challenge in your teen years?

How did you overcome this?

Who has been your biggest influence and why? Have you told them what they meant to you? If not, have you thought about telling them, and are you going to?

Where, or from whom, did you learn respect for authority? What does this mean to you?

Chapter Five

FINDING CHRIST

*"A man found him wandering around in the fields and asked him,
'What are you looking for?'"(Genesis 37:15, NIV)*

*"I remember my affliction and my wandering,
the bitterness and the gall."(Lamentations 3:19, NIV)*

I used to walk my dog (Juno) every day, and I always used those times for prayer and giving thanks for what I have and what I have become. I have since traded my walks for time on my knees in my living room with worship music and coffee. I had to give Juno back to her original owner because my life became too busy to properly care for her.

I think about my life during this prayer time and reflect on what God has done for me, even when I couldn't see Him. I understand the importance of this time with my Father. I am able to get focused on what it is He wants me to do and has planned for me to do during the day, and when I don't spend this time with Him (which happens from time to time), my day is filled with confusion and turmoil.

I felt for some time that I was in a spiritual tug of war for my soul, and even expressed this to Christina during one of my counseling sessions. I believe we all are in this fight every day, no matter where we come from or where we are in our walk. I started understanding this more and more after finding the teaching of Rick Warren.

My reason for this belief is that I walked hand and hand with Satan for over thirty years. Then I started seeing Christ, and I started seeing the light, but every time I stepped into Christ, Satan would pull me back by using my former life and temptations. Due to my lack of spiritual strength, I was repeatedly finding myself back on his side of the war.

Understanding Sin, Transgression, and Iniquity has helped me become more aware of this dynamic. Now I am able to fight off the temptations a little better. I still stumble sometimes, just like we all do, but the "fall" is not so far now. As I was writing this, Psalm 51:10 came to me, "Create in me a clean heart, O God. Renew a loyal spirit within me." I so needed this right now.

As I started researching my family and my story, I started uncovering things that were very unsettling to me. I let it affect me to the point that it spilled out of me and affected those around me, like in the past. This is one of the biggest fights that I have with my old self and my temper.

One thing I have learned is that after you give your life to Christ, you are saved, but your journey is just starting. You can start fresh because you have a NEW you. However, the war between your old self and your new self will rage, and as you grow stronger, the battles become less and less. But, as Paul said in Romans in 7:15, "I do not understand myself. I want to do what is right, but I do not do it. Instead, I do the very thing I hate." And this is my life; even today it's a daily battle.

When God tells us to do something and we don't, we are in a war with God. I have been in this war for years because I wanted to do what *I* wanted; not what *God* wanted me to do. I think this came from having to stand up to my dad at the age of twelve to get him to stop beating up my mom and me. As Christina said, I put on armor that was so strong that I wouldn't let anyone see me, including God. I took this newfound power and used it for myself and myself alone for years, not understanding that this power should have been used for God's plan, not John's.

This epiphany didn't come to me until hearing the message from Pastor Rick Warren, entitled, "Why Is Life in This World So Hard?" In the message, he outlines the three types of rebellion, which are:

1. **Sin:** I want what I want; sin is falling short or missing the mark. I am inadequate to be perfect. We all fall short of perfection, which is called sin.
2. **Transgression:** This means you go too far, go past the boundary, you break the law; it is an intentional disobedience.
3. **Iniquity:** This is an intention to hurt, damage, or to do evil because you are mad, jealous, prideful, envious, bitter, or someone has offended you and you want to hurt them back—intentionally hurting someone.

Why was this so meaningful to me? It opened up clarity to where I had made my mistake. I am now a believer that when you own the mistakes you have made, it then becomes easier to correct them and not make them again. Most of my rebellions would be placed under the category of "transgression," with some falling into the "iniquity" category, because I know that in my past I hurt some individuals and I would have to say that some were very intentional. To help you understand this better, I offer Rick Warren's football analogy on the three types of rebellion, because it helped me better understand them:

> *"If I am in a football game and I want to know the difference between a sin, a transgression, and an iniquity, a sin would be kicking a field goal and it misses; it falls short, or it hit the crossbar. That is a sin: I've missed the mark; I fell short. A transgression would be offsides: if I jump offside before the snap is taken in football, I intentionally was going after you; I'm offsides. If I go out of bounds with the ball, that's not a sin, that's a transgression. I've gone out of bounds; I've broken the law; the law says you stay within these boundaries if you are playing football. An iniquity would be if I come up and head butt you or kick you in the face and I break your... that's a personal foul. That's an iniquity; I want to intentionally hurt you I want to take you out of the game."*

I hope this helps you understand these three rebellions the same way it did for me. This really cleared up the way I look back on my past and has put a new light on forgiving myself and understanding the forgiveness that our Father has for us. We break God's Laws, and sin has broken the world, and that is why nothing works correctly. Boy was this eye opening! We all have freedom of choice. I made some bad choices, but if I had been right with the Father then those choices wouldn't have been there to be made. One of my assistant coaches once told our team the following: "We have been where you are, you haven't been where we are, so learn from us." That is part of what I am trying to do by writing this book. Learn from my mistakes, my sins, my transgressions, and my iniquities.

"The Lord is my shepherd I'm following him,
not perfectly, but increasingly.
I'm not what I could be,
I'm not what I should be.
But I'm not what I was.
There is a growing pattern of obedience and faith."
~James McDonald

"Surely the arm of the Lord is not too short to save,
nor his ears to dull to hear.
But your iniquities have separated you from your God;
your sins have hidden his face from you, so that he will not hear."
(Isaiah 59:1-2, NIV)

Boot Camp

Back to the point in my life where I felt there was something more than the drugs and partying. I needed to escape from that life and start a new one. I started thinking about coaching so I could help kids with similar childhoods to my own not make the mistakes I did. I must say that the thought of coaching had been with me for a while before I joined the Corps. That is part of the reason I joined the Corps, so I could get money through the GI Bill to go to college.

So, I joined the Marine Corps, which most likely saved my life. If I would have stayed in that life I was living, I would likely have ended up dead or in jail. This was the start of my long journey to finding Christ, and then growing and maturing into the Christian man I am today.

On March 3, 1987, I headed to Sea-Tac Airport to fly to MCRD San Diego to spend the next three months in boot camp. Prior to this trip, I had been working with the local recruiters to be as ready as I could be. I had no idea what to expect when the plane landed in San Diego. All I know is that I wanted out of Renton and wanted to get through the next four years so I could go to school and become a P.E. teacher and coach.

I can still recall the first day of boot camp like it was yesterday. (For those of you who have served, you know what I am saying.) The bus rolls to a stop, the doors open, and on to the bus steps a Drill Instructor (DI). He shouts, "From now on, the first and last words out of your mouth with be, 'Sir!'—is that clear?"

The busload of recruits answered, "Sir, yes, sir!"

He shouted, "I CAN'T HEAR YOU!"

"SIR, YES, SIR!" we shouted back.

He then said, "When I say move, I want you to get your #%$ off this bus and line up on the yellow footprints. Is that clear?"

"Sir, yes, sir!" we cried.

"What are you still doing on my bus?" he shouted.

There was a mad scramble as we tried to get off the bus as fast as we could and get into formation on the perfectly placed footprints. The training had started. As we stood in our first formation, the DI moved through the group as if they were looking for someone or just simply looking us over to see what they had to mold into Marines over the next three months. One of them was shouting commands to us, about how we were going in to get our hair cut, better yet shaved to the skull. All of a sudden, he stopped. It was dead quiet and none of us moved at all. Then from the quiet came, "OH MY GOD; IT IS JESUS CHRIST HIMSELF!"

There was one recruit who had hair down to his shoulders. I had cut my hair prior to leaving. It was not as short as they were going to cut it in boot camp, but I didn't arrive with the big curly long hair that I'd previously had. Then the DI said, "Come on, boy, you are going to the front of the line." I knew that everyone was watching this event, although I didn't look around. The young man was escorted into the building only to exit moments later with what looked like a "five o'clock shadow" length haircut.

Haircuts complete, we moved to uniform issue and turned in all of the civilian things we had. Then off to the barracks. I won't bore you with three months of boot camp stories. But I will share one.

While in boot camp, I attended my first church service. I wish I could tell you that I attended church because I wanted to know about Christ, but the first Sunday I just wanted to get a break away from the DI's. It was the only time during the week that we could have a break. How about God using that to start my journey? We have all heard that God works in mysterious ways—it's true! I came across this in one of my readings: "God meets us where we are. God comes to us in ways that we can understand and appreciate, even if only partially or incompletely" (James McDonald). I believe this was God coming to me where I was, even though the work was incomplete at the time the seed was planted.

After three days, we received the news that our DIs would be with us for the rest of our time. For me, boot camp was not any more physically demanding than football two-a-days. I found it more mentally demanding. About halfway through camp is when I figured out what the game was. The DIs were putting us into situations that were chaotic and stressful to see who would step up and who wasn't ready to be a Marine. I graduated with most of the men I started camp with; a few didn't make it all the way through and were recycled back into a platoon behind us to go through that part of camp over again.

My dad and stepmom attended my graduation, and this was the first time I had seen my dad in a while. We spent the weekend together, then I was off to my first duty station in Maryland, where I spent the next five months in school learning how to work on howitzers. Then it was off to Okinawa, Japan for a year.

When I arrived in Okinawa, I was only there a few days, then I was sent to Korea to catch up with the unit I was to be with for the remainder of my time in Okinawa. We spent three months in Korea, in "tent city." (I compare this to the show *M.A.S.H* for those of you from my generation; you will understand that comparison.) During my time overseas, I did not attend any church services; most of my time was spent golfing and partying. I had never played golf until then and I became obsessed with the game (which I continue to play to this day). After Okinawa, I was sent to 29 Palms, California, where I would spend the remainder of my time in the Corps.

During my time overseas I started thinking of all the things my mom had told us growing up: things like Dad wasn't sending money to help, that Dad was fighting her on child support, and things she told us about MamaDel and PapaChub's trust fund. I wanted to have those questions answered. Growing up, I only had her side of the story. I knew the beatings were real, but I could only take her word on the rest. Mom's bitterness was justified but she needed to forgive so she could be free from that, which, sadly, was something she never did.

RELFECTION or DISCUSSION

Are there ways you can see that you have wandered in your life and walk with God?

In what ways does Pastor Rick Warren's message, mentioned in this chapter, help you understand sin, transgression, and iniquity?

What choices have you made in your life that you would now consider "bad" ones?

What has been the biggest turning point in your life other than accepting Jesus?

Explain what repentance means to you.

Is there anything you feel the Holy Spirit calling you to repent of? I encourage you to take that step now. (If you are in a group, you can ask for their support as you pray.)

Chapter Six

THE FALL

"The sin of humanity is that it grabbed at the beautiful Thing—a piece of fruit that was 'pleasing to the eye'— rather than trusting what God has said."
~ A.J. Swoboda

When I returned from Okinawa, I went to Colorado, where my dad was living. I arrived unannounced on his doorstep; he had no idea I was coming. I knocked on the door and then braced myself to punch him in the mouth if he answered the door. The door opened and—bam—I hit him square on the jaw. He fell to the ground and got up wiping the blood off his lip. He simply said, "I deserved that. Let's have a beer and talk." We went downstairs and talked for hours.

During this talk, I found out that some of the things my mom had been telling us weren't true, which was upsetting. Angry, I then flew home to talk to my mom. This wasn't easy, but I had to confront her with what I'd discovered. Her initial reaction was to continue to lie but I put a stop to that. When I asked her why she did it she had no answer.

After we talked for a while, I told her she needed to tell my brothers the truth, and that she needed to stop lying. During our childhood, Mom had tended to brag about me to the point it hardened my brother's heart toward me. I didn't realize the extent of this until after she was gone. It wasn't until Jason was living with me that I truly saw the effects of this on him and the strain it had placed on our relationship.

Now that I had some of my family issues cleared up, I was on my way to 29 Palms. Had I known then what I know now about my arm injury, I would have dug deeper into that then.

Moving On

I arrived in 29 Palms at night. I remember thinking, *This can't be as bad as everyone was saying,* but seeing the Stumps at night was a bit deceiving. When I woke up and stepped outside the next morning, I thought, *Oh my. I am in the desert.* Still having not been back to a church service since boot camp, I had remained a wanderer. Now I was in the desert literally.

It is here that I met my wife of nine years, Lynn. A fellow Marine and close friend was dating her roommate, and we were all going to the drive-in movies that night. She was a first-grade teacher there in 29 Palms; she and a friend had moved there from Ohio about the same time I arrived. We started dating shortly after that night.

This is also where I started my coaching career, starting with coaching my unit's eight-man football team. Yes, I said eight-man—it was full contact, played on an eighty-yard field. It was a speed game. It was interesting developing plays, but at the same time it was preparing me for my career. I then moved to the local high school for my first high school coaching job as the varsity linebacker's coach. I would also work spring breaks in Palm Springs as a bouncer during my time there. This was how I spent most of my time in the Stumps.

This was mostly how the time passed until February of '91, when I was due to be discharged in March. However, Iraq had invaded Kuwait and Desert Storm had started. Some of my unit was already being sent overseas.

My boss came into the armory and said that he had good news and bad news; which did I want to hear first? I said, "Give me the bad."

He said, "You won't be able to be discharged until everyone comes home."

I replied, "Okay, what's the good news?

"You won't be going over there; you have been deemed 'tag mission essential United States,'" he said. With that news, I had no idea when I would be getting out. Lynn and I were planning on getting married after I was out of the Corps, and I knew we could only go to one of two places: Ohio University or the University of Washington.

I was accepted at Ohio U and after I was finally discharged we moved back to Athens, Ohio, and moved in with Lynn's mom until we could get our own place. We were married in June of the following year. I was able to get a job coaching at the high school in town while working on my bachelor's degree. Starting college at the age of twenty-seven was a bit different, and since

I was someone who had not taken high school seriously, I had to learn how to study. My mindset was totally different toward school now. The Marines had changed me, and I was paying for school now, so I was going to get the most out of it. Plus, I was going to school to be a coach and teacher. It wasn't easy and I owe a lot to Lynn for her support and help through those years.

I graduated Cum Laude with a bachelor's degree in physical education. As I was finishing, the Ohio football staff went through a coaching change. Coincidentally, the new head coach's sons played for the school where I was coaching. Through this connection, I was able to get a graduate assistant position on his staff at the university. I moved directly into my master's program and coaching.

Over the following two years I learned more about football than I could have imagined—not only the X's and O's but how to run a program. I thank Coach Grobe and the rest of the staff for that opportunity, and to this day I model a lot of what I learned from those days at Ohio.

It wasn't easy going to school and coaching during the football season. I was up early, into the offices, then to class, then back to pre-practice meetings, practice, film cut up, then homework. Then when games started, this was seven days a week to stay on top of everything I had to do. In '97, I graduated with a Master of Science in P.E./Athletic Administration, with honors again. (I only mention this to say that people do change and can change. However, I would still fall, as you will see. But to go from being a kid with dyslexia and who cared nothing about school to graduating with honors says something, and I hope that might help someone reading this to understand that *you* can overcome too.)

This is also around the time I found out that I could not have children. This was devastating news to me. I wanted nothing more than to have a son whom I could bring to games with me and eventually coach one day. But for some reason, it was not in God's plan for me. I may never know why, and I wish I would have had the faith I have now back then.

As I look back on this time I wish I would have sought out counseling. This deep disappointment would haunt me for a while. In his book, *The Glorious Dark*, A.J. Swoboda says, "Infertility is that kind of hell for many. Because every time someone asks if you're going to have kids someday," (or in my case do you have kids), "you're reminded of the sign above your head. It doesn't go away." It wasn't until I developed a deeper faith and grew older that this did not bother me. It is God's will and I accept that now. Something good will and has come from this.

A Coaching Career

After graduating, I took a job as the Athletic Director (AD) and Defensive Coordinator (DC) at St. Stephens High in North Carolina. It was an interesting situation being the AD and then the DC on the football staff. We were taking over a school that had not been in the playoffs for ten seasons. After the first season, the principal made a coaching change, and I became the Head Coach (HC). So, one year out of college, I was now the AD/HC.

Trying to rebuild a football program is always hard. One way I did this is with "The Sledgehammer." It was an authentic, sixteen-pound sledgehammer, whose shaft I had the art teacher paint in school colors with the following words: "1998 St. Stephens Sledgehammer Award." (Today everyone sees the turnover chain or belt that colleges hand out when someone gets a turnover. I would like to think that we had a hand in starting this trend.)

The Sledgehammer was given to the player who had the biggest hit in the game. You see, I needed to teach my kids how to be physical, and this seemed like a good way to do it. It turned out to be that key, though some of the hammer quals (this is what we called a hit worthy of the Hammer) might not be allowed in today's football. The winner each week got to keep the hammer in their locker and then carry it onto the field during pre-game, and onto the bus if we played on the road. This changed the mindset of our team. I brought the Hammer to every program after that.

I was at St. Stephens for six years. The staff and I did turn the program around and had success over this time. Sadly, my sense of success was setting me up for a fall.

This was my first big transgression and fall since my younger years. I don't want to go too far into the details of the events out of respect for those involved and those I hurt. If you are reading this and happen to be one of those family members, coaches, teachers, players, and friends in my life during this time, please forgive me for this. That was a tough time for all of us. Those events will stay with me forever. They are the reason Lynn and I are no longer together, because of my infidelity.

My transgression was public. The mental and physical pain on me and others was huge. Just dealing with the publicity of it, and the stress, and the mental fatigue, put me in the hospital. And then, when it became clear I could no longer lead the high school football team with the same integrity I had before, I knew I needed to move.

I was going to relocate right away, but my principal at the time convinced me to stay one more year; however, I knew I needed to move on, and they needed a new leader. So, I started looking for a new school. I ended up moving to Cairo, Georgia, where I stayed for two short years. You will see why as you read on. For now, though, I need to circle back to my dad.

Too-Soon Goodbye

My dad passed in 2003 while I was coaching at Cairo High. I will never forget that day. I was at a wedding when I received the call from my stepmother. She would call from time to time because my dad would be acting like a fool and I would talk to Dad and help him through whatever it was. Then he would settle down, with apologies, and they would move on. I listened to her voicemail as soon as I could: "John I need to talk to you about your dad." I thought, *What has he done now?*

So I called, and she picked up. "John, your dad is gone," she said after our hellos.

"He left you?" I said.

She repeated, "Your dad is gone."

Again, I repeated, "What do you mean—did he leave you?"

"No," she said quietly. "He died, John."

I couldn't believe what I'd just heard. She went on to tell me what had happened. Dad was mowing the yard, came in, and asked for a glass of tea. When she came to the living room with the tea, dad was gone. He'd had a heart attack that day.

From the day I punched him, my relationship with my dad changed. We would talk every Sunday morning until he was taken Home. The first Sunday after Dad passed and a number of them over the next few months, were tough, not getting that call in the early morning. My dad and stepmom were raising one of her grandchildren because one of her daughters was a heroin user and had died on the delivery table giving birth. I always looked at this as my dad's second chance. He loved that young man as if he was his own son.

This was a long week; we were still in season and were preparing for a game on the upcoming Friday night. I went that day to my head coaches and told them what had happened and that I needed to go to Colorado for the service. The rest of the day was spent simultaneously booking a flight and looking at game film of our upcoming opponent. (I couldn't get a flight out until the next day, so watching game film was a way to take my mind off things.) Then it was off to Colorado for Dad's service.

My return flight was on game day. I was hoping to be back before kickoff, which I just missed if my memory is correct. I pushed the speed limits and arrived at the stadium to find a parking spot that had been held for me right in front of the stadium. I went through the offices and down onto the game field to the warmest welcome that one could have. The team had decided to wear our all-black uniforms that night to honor my dad. These uniforms are not worn that often, so this was a true honor, something I will never forget.

RELFECTION or DISCUSSION

What are some of your own sins, transgressions, and iniquities? Can you differentiate between them, based on the definitions in this chapter?

Looking back on these, did any of them cause you loss?

Have you sought forgiveness? If yes, what was the outcome? If not, why not?

Have you lost a close family member or friend? If so, how did you grieve?

Chapter Seven

HOMECOMING

"God's supreme purpose for us is to make us like His Son, Jesus Christ. If we understand that everything happening to us is to make us more Christlike, it will solve a great deal of anxiety in our lives."

~ A.W. Tozer

That Christmas I went home to Seattle to see the family. It was the first time in eighteen years that I wasn't ready to leave at the end of my visit. Mom wasn't doing well and, having lost Dad, I realized I needed to move home to be around the family. When I returned to Cairo, I went straight to Coach's house and gave him the bad news that I would be moving home.

After applying for a few jobs in the Seattle area, I went back home for interviews. I landed a position at a high school that had not won a game in twenty-eight games—the longest current losing streak in Washington. I took it.

My first priority was finding a coach who could run study tables while I was back in Georgia finishing out the year. The good news was that I found two, and I met with both of them before I returned to Cairo. There was a major academic problem on this new team; only about 50 percent of the players had grades good enough to allow them to play. We had to start study hall as soon as possible. By the time I returned in the summer, we had about 85 percent of the players eligible to play in the upcoming year.

Coming Home

When the time came to move, my trip from Georgia to Seattle was a coach's dream trip. I was driving the 2500-plus miles, so I got out a map and took a look at what colleges I could stop at along the way. Once I had the route in place, it was drive for a day, stay the night, then meet with the college staff to go over their offense or defense, based on which college I was at. All the stops had to be running our schemes or something very similar. My new OC flew down to Oklahoma and joined me on the trip and it was one of the best trips I could have had. We learned so much and ended up implementing a lot of the information we learned. We stopped at Memphis, Oklahoma, Air Force, Utah, and Boise State.

Midway through our first season, we still needed a win to break the losing streak and we finally secured our first win in game six. I could now breathe a sigh of relief that my name would not be attached to the longest losing streak in the history of the State of Washington.

It was here that I started attending church on a regular basis. My linebacker coach was a pastor of a local church, and with a request from the players, we also started an FCA huddle (Fellowship of Christian Athletes) at the school. I would end up getting my mom and my brother to attend church with me, which was something I never thought would happen. This was the first time I accepted Christ into my life. (I correctly called this "the first time," and you will understand why later.)

Even as I accepted Christ, my old self was still stronger than my faith, and I would fall once again. I stayed at this school until '05, then I made my final coaching change. I left after two years and moved into the personal training field. In retrospect, I can see the pattern now. When I would start having success, I would sabotage it, and it caused me to have to move.

I ended up losing Mom in '08. It was December and David called me with the news. I jumped in the car and drove to pick up Jason and Jessica and headed to the hospital in downtown Seattle. By the time we got there, she was gone. We sat around for a while and then headed to Dave's place. We were up all night that night.

Seeking Help

By this time, I had already made the transition to the training industry and was working at a fitness club in Tacoma. When I moved to Tacoma, I stopped attending church and didn't really read the Bible much anymore. I was seeing the self-sabotage starting over again and it was bad, worse than ever before. I knew I needed help. As author James MacDonald said in his book, *Act Like Men,* ". . . my awareness of when I might be tempted so I can avoid the situation altogether has become acute."[10]

---

10 MacDonald, James, and Gene A. Getz. *Act like Men.* Chicago: Moody Publishers, 2014.

I made the choice to find a counselor. I knew I needed someone who wouldn't judge me and condemn me for my behavior. I had been in counseling before, so I knew what I was looking for. So, I opened a Google search and started calling; the first two weren't taking new clients. However, the third was, and this was a "God Thing." It was Christina. We would work together for ten-plus years.

I can say because of this work I am free now. I owe Christina my life. I want to let you, the reader, know that going to a counselor is not a bad thing. So many people feel this way. My brother Steve used to tell me he was hesitant to go to a counselor because he didn't want people to think he was crazy. I told him, "Sorry, bro, you *are* crazy, and so am I; we are all a bit crazy."

In 2012, the fitness club where I was working was bought by a larger company and I didn't want to work for them. So, I did want I had been wanting to do for a while: I opened my own gym, Summit Strength & Conditioning. I spent months researching how to write a business plan and what makes a small business succeed or fail. I put together my plan and presented it to two of my clients. Both invested in my idea, and I owe them a lot.

Dusty ended up as my partner. He was the business brains and I focused on getting clients and building the business. I learned so much from this man. I could not have had a better partner. Our friendship never faltered, and we remain close friends to this day. I can count on one hand the confrontations that we had. Looking back on our seven years, the only regret we both have is opening a second location. When we saw how badly the gym was doing financially, we should have run and run fast from that. Looking back, I realize we let our egos get the best of us. We stayed, and we made some progress, but we never really got it going. We ended up shutting it down and went back to one gym. Even with doing this, we never really recovered.

More Loss

I lost my brother Dave on January 16, 2013. Next to losing my dad, this was a big loss to me. Dave had a heart attack while at work, and on the 14th I got the call. When I arrived at the hospital, he was hooked up to life support and it didn't look good.

While at work, Dave had gone outside for lunch and when he didn't return, his co-workers called him, with no answer. They waited for a bit, then they went to look for him—they found him in his truck unconscious and with no pulse. When the EMTs showed up, they were able to get his heart started, so it couldn't have been more than ten or fifteen minutes.

The doctors told me they were going to perform a CT scan the following day to check for brain activity. We were all there in his room, and his stepdaughter looked at me and said, "Oh my god, John; it's your birthday." Yes, that day was my birthday.

I looked at her and just said, "It's okay."

When I left that night, I reflected on the doctors' recommendation of a CT scan. They told me that when the EMTs had arrived at Dave's workplace, when they initially responded to the 911 call, they had immediately started a procedure known as "Therapeutic Hypothermia." I felt prompted to look into this more, and discovered it was a new technology that places the patient in a hypothermic state so that the blood flow is directed to the vital organs. The procedure was successful when the patient was found in time and, as I said, we did not know how long

Dave had been without oxygen. If he had been found in time, it was possible he could still have a chance at life.

The next day, I headed back to Bellevue and Overlake Hospital. When I arrived, the scan was being conducted to check for brain activity. The next day, the test came back showing no brain activity. Dave was gone.

Now the choice came: to keep him on life support or take him off. I knew that he would not want to stay on the support. I said my goodbyes to him and then told his wife that I would not be coming back up; I didn't want to see him again like this. It was her choice to make, and I would understand whatever one she made. She told me she couldn't make the call.

I asked, "Do you mean taking him off or telling the doctors? "She told me she couldn't tell the doctors to take him off the life support, so I said, "When you are ready, let me know, and I will call the doctors and tell them." Then I left for home.

As I was driving back, I received a call saying that Dave had passed. I was surprised at first, then I asked, "How long did he stay with us after they turned the machines off?"

"Just a few minutes," was the answer.

Dave was now home.

It was January 16, 2013, but I will always say the 15th. Here is another "God Thing." Dave liked bald eagles and this country more than most. Shortly after his service, I was playing golf at Chambers Bay in University Place, Washington, and heading up the tenth fairway I looked to my right and there on the hill sat a bald eagle. I thought, *How cool is that?* I went on to finish the tenth hole, and when I got to number twelve, there was the eagle again. Heading to the fifteenth hole, I see the eagle in the only tree at Chambers Bay. Then he was on the eighteenth as I finished my round. To this day, almost every time I play a round of golf, I see an eagle on or flying over the course. It makes me feel like Dave is with me, even though he rarely played golf himself.

On Eagle's Wings

The Bible tells us that ". . . like a parent eagle tenderly meeting every need, so the Lord of hosts hovers over his people, protects us (Isaiah 31:5), provides for our every need (Philippians 4:19), and never, ever leaves or forsakes us (Deuteronomy 31:6)." [11]

According to traditional Native American beliefs, the Creator made all the birds of the sky when the World was new. Of all the birds, the Creator chose the eagle to be the leader... the Master of the Sky. The Native American tradition believes that, because the eagle flies higher and sees better than any other bird, its perspective is different from other creations that are held close to the earth, and it is, therefore, closer to the Creator. The Creator also has a different perspective of what occurs below in this world of physical things in which humankind resides. The eagle spends more time in the higher element of Father Sky than other birds, and Father Sky is an element of the Spirit. [12]

In the Bible, we read, "But those who trust in the Lord will find new strength. They will soar high on wings like eagles. They will run and not grow weary. They will walk and not faint" (Isaiah 40:31). Author Michael Bradley, in his article, "Traits of the

---

11 Ryan Duncan, "What Do Eagles Have to Teach Us about God?," Crosswalk. com (Salem Web Network, June 13, 2017), https://www.crosswalk.com/blogs/ christian-trends/what-do-eagles-have-to-teach-us-about-god.html.

12 www.eagles.org/what-we-do/eductate/learn-about-eagles/bald-eagles/usas-national-symbol/

Eagle and How It Pertains to Our Christian Walk," does a great job describing the eagle's qualities and how they relate to us. He points out that we are the eagle. The wings of the eagle represent our faith and belief in God. The wind thermals that the eagle fly on represent the Holy Spirit.. Bottom line: if we do not have enough faith and belief in God to take flight on the Holy Spirit in order to be led and empowered by Him for service to the Lord, then nothing will ever happen. We will forever stay perched, and we will never fulfill the divine destiny God has already planned out for our lives before we were even conceived in our mother's womb.

The eagle has to take that big leap off the edge of the cliff in order to be able to fly and soar on those wind thermals. If the eagle does not take flight on those wind thermals, when they do come up on him, he will forever stay perched and will die on the cliff of starvation.

In the same way, if we do not take flight on the Holy Spirit and the divine call God has placed on our lives, our lives will perish right before our very eyes, as the Bible tells us that God's people will perish without having His specific vision for their lives.

Eagles are also considered master fishermen. They are very good at locking in on their prey and then swooping down to catch it. How many times have you seen videos where an eagle will swoop down on a body of water and pick up a fish swimming near the surface with perfect ease and accuracy, catching them on the very first attempt? They are absolute masters at hunting down and catching their prey, whether that prey be on land or in the water.

Just as eagles are considered to be master fishermen with how they can catch fish in water, we, as Christians, have been called by the Lord to be "fishers of men," just like Jesus and the apostles were at the very beginning of the New Testament.

Our number one job in this life is to try and get as many people saved as we possibly can.

Personal evangelism within our own circle of influence is something that each and every Christian can do for the Lord, and it is something that we should always be on the alert for. You never know when the Holy Spirit will move you to lead you to someone He will want you to share your faith with, whether it be someone you might know or a complete stranger.[13]

Our wandering continues no matter how mature we become. It's part of the walk. It was never promised to be a smooth ride. We are going to be on the mountain tops, and then in the valleys. Psalms tells us this. But, like eagles, we can rise up, with God's help.

The struggles of my valleys are where we are going next. What I've learned from them is that it is easy to praise God when we are on the top, but what we really need to learn is how to praise Him in the valleys as well. The valleys are where growth happens.

RELFECTION or DISCUSSION

Have you ever experienced the loss of a close friend or family member? How has this affected your view or relationship with God? Has it strengthened it or weakened it?

---

13 Ryan Duncan, "What Do Eagles Have to Teach Us about God?," Crosswalk. com (Salem Web Network, June 13, 2017), https://www.crosswalk.com/blogs/ christian-trends/what-do-eagles-have-to-teach-us-about-god.html.

Have you been mad at God? If so, over what and how did you resolve this feeling?

I believe the eagles I saw were a "sign" from God and drove me to His Word and character in very personally meaningful ways. Have you ever had any "God Things" that moved you in this way?

Chapter Eight

THE STRUGGLE

"If you lay a hand on it, you will remember the struggle and never do it again." (Job 41:8, NIV)

I was driving to work one day, frustrated with where my life was going and feeling as if God was punishing me for my past. I am sure many of you have felt the same and maybe still do. I can tell you, that is not the case. God doesn't punish; He tests and disciplines us just as our earthly fathers do. I didn't understand this until now.

On this day, I was driving to work, I was crying out to God, I was yelling at the top of my lungs asking, "GOD, WHY, WHY ME? WHY ARE YOU DOING THIS TO ME!?" After I calmed down a bit, I told God if he brought a Christian woman into my life, I would start walking the walk. I believe it's okay to be mad at God; He even says that He is slow to anger (Psalm 103:8), so if He made us in His image, then we can have the emotion of anger, even toward Him. However, I was placing the blame in the wrong place. God was not to blame for what I was going through, I was. I needed to find myself. At this time in my life, I was still in destruction mode, and I was way out of control.

Shortly after this, I was at a networking event, and I saw Leah. Later, we were seated at the same table, so through the mornings' networking, I learned a bit about her. After the event, I asked her out for dinner, and she accepted. A few dates later, we decided to make it official and start dating.

A Biblical Relationship

I will always remember Leah saying, "I just want you to know that I am not going to sleep with you." I have to say I was a bit shocked by this; I had never had a woman say something like this before. As we continued to talk about our expectations of what our relationship were, we made a commitment to one another that our relationship would be based on biblical principles. We did just that, for the four years we were together, and we modeled the best we could a godly relationship in every way. I can tell you that we never slept together; we were going to wait until we were married if that was God's plan.

Now, I know what you are thinking. You are thinking the same thing everyone else thought when I or we would tell them that. But it's true, and this was a life changer for me (those of you who know me from my past life will know that). I had never experienced a biblical relationship before.

I started back to church with Leah and that ended up being one of the best things ever. This is where I meet Scotty Kessler, my spiritual mentor, and Eric Boles, a pastor, brother, and teacher in Christ. I started ushering at church with Leah to get more involved in the church family. This was God working in my life. My growth as a Christian during my time with Leah was second only to the growth I experienced in seminary. She helped me learn what it was to walk in the light of our Father. She helped me, along with Christina, to become vulnerable.

If I learned one thing during this time, it is that when you start walking with Christ it makes you start looking at yourself. In his book *A Glorious Dark*, A.J. Swoboda makes the following statement:

> *"Christianity forced me to deal with the evil inside me. I don't question that evil is out there in the world. Evil is out there. It's also in here. I see evil almost everywhere—in music, in culture, in art, in religion. Evil is out there. But by externalizing the darkness, we inherently internalize the light. By that I mean that to the degree we see evil all around us we are too often less likely to see it in ourselves. Or to put it more simply, we externalize the cause of darkness and internalize the consequences of darkness. This is the root of hypocrisy: the unwillingness to see the darkness inside ourselves. Christianity doesn't allow us to externalize darkness. It forces us to deal with the darkness inside our own hearts."[14]*

---

14 Swoboda, A. J. *A Glorious Dark: Finding Hope in the Tension between Belief and Experience*. Grand Rapids: Baker Books, 2015.

After reading this, I realized I needed to not only look at the darkness within me, but I also need to work to get rid of the darkness. Over the next few years, I would do just that.

Why Is Life So Messy?

Looking back at everything I did in my life; it was easy to see the darkness. The good news is that, through Christ, we are redeemed. The tough part is conducting the self-examination so that we can empty our hearts and grow closer to Jesus through sanctification. This was echoed by A.W. Tozer, who wrote, "The ancient curse will not go out painlessly; the tough old miser within us will not lie down and die obedient to our command. He must be torn out of our heart like a plant from the soil; he must be extracted in agony and blood like a tooth from the jaw." [15]

This is when I start journaling. After I hit my knees, I would journal daily for over a year. I haven't journaled since then, but I believe that journaling helped me through this season, and it allowed me to see God's work in my life during a storm. When I journaled, I followed the following format: I would start with praise, then prayers, then evidence of God, then the day. This helped me see the darkness in and around me, and also helped me see the goodness of God's work in and around me. The struggle is real and we as Christians' face it daily.

In A.J. Swoboda's first book, *Messy,* he said, "My life is messier after I started following the Jesus I met than it was

---

15   Tozer, A. W. *The Pursuit of God: The Human Thirst for the Divine.* Chicago: Moody Publishers, 2015.

before."[16] I believe this mess is because of the self-examination we must go through, and as we mature we are tested, disciplined, and attacked. Christianity is not a bed of roses. It's more like the thorns on the roses: we get scraped, poked, cut, and bleed.

One of the hardest things to see in our new walk is seeing people fall that we never thought would we see fall. What I learned from this is that we can't place the people in the ministry or the buildings we go to on the same level as Jesus. Humans will disappoint; the question is what to do when that happens. Some of the people I have learned from, and that I have quoted in this book, have fallen. That doesn't mean that their teaching was not valid; it simply means they are flawed like the rest of us. And that's why I choose to use their teaching still. We not only learn from a fall, but we can also teach from a fall as well.

Some call these falls a test, others say a storm, others say a season, or trials, but "detours" was one of my favorites. Tony Evans called them detours. He said it this way, "When they are doing road construction, they put up a detour sign for you to go another way while the construction is taking place."[17] So, when you are going through the struggle, seek God because He is using this to prepare you for something. He is molding you for His purpose. Once we understand this, it becomes easier to just rest in faith rather than trying to get in the way of the plan God has for us.

---

16 Swoboda, A. J. *Messy: God Likes It That Way.* Grand Rapids, MI: Kregel Publications, 2012.

17 Evans, Tony. *Detours: The Unpredictable Path to Your Destiny.* Nashville, TN: B & H Publishing Group, 2017.

Learning to Be Vulnerable

One day in my morning reading, I came to 2 Corinthians 12:8-10 (NIV):

> *"Three times I pleaded with the Lord to take it away from me. But he said to me, 'My grace is sufficient for you, for my power is made perfect in weakness.' Therefore I will boast all the more gladly about my weaknesses, so that Christ's power may rest on me. That is why, for Christ's sake, I delight in weakness, in insults, in hardship, in persecutions, in difficulties. For when I am weak, then I am strong."*

Weakness is another big struggle I had. I never wanted to feel weak or wanted to be seen as weak. Growing up, I had to be strong, so this word wasn't even in my vocabulary. The biblical use of this word doesn't mean weak physically, my thinking was that it did. The reality is, I discovered that, as Christians, we have to be vulnerable—this word was foreign to me! In my first fifty years, I never showed any vulnerability. I didn't let anyone in. This prevented me from having what I now know is unconditional true love.

I lived in the past without vulnerability. When you truly love, you become vulnerable. This is true in our love for Christ and His love for us. This was something Christina was working with me on. For years, this was a recurring theme in our sessions, and it took years to get me there.

I realize now that you can be saved, but it's a relationship, and just as in any relationship it's a two-way street. Both people in a relationship MUST be active, and because God wants to be active in our life, we must be active in our relationship with Him. He revealed to me that I had to start doing my part.

As I was in this storm, I came across a song by Ryan Stevenson, called "In the Eye of the Storm." I played this song daily. But my prideful ignorance kept me from having true spiritual insight. I stood before the Lord guilty but wouldn't admit or recognize it. This came to me one morning in prayer.

I quickly learned that prayer is listening, but to hear the Spirit you need to completely surrender. I was reading 2 Corinthians 3:18 one morning and, after reading my notes, I heard the Spirit say, *John, your veil has been removed, now you can see and reflect the glory of the Lord. And the Lord, who is the Spirit, makes you more and more like Him as you are changed into His glorious image. Sanctification takes a lifetime; you are being changed daily and you won't be complete until you are in your Father's house.*

Christina would always refer to a child in our sessions. A thought came to mind about the child that we always talked about. My shame and anger were built up from the fact that I couldn't do anything to stop whatever took place, or in any way help this child. When I "saw" that child Christina described, sitting on the side of the road (in my mind's eye), I looked the other way because I didn't help him when I could have. (Christina, you will be happy to know I would now stop and help this child and then give him the hug you know I couldn't give him before.) Learning to love this child was a great step in learning to be vulnerable.

Growing in Faith and Service

Through the storm of closing our second fitness center location, I began to serve more at church. Having the fellowship of the church during this time helped me get through the trial and strengthened my faith. This was the first time I really felt that I let people help me. Before this, I used to try to do everything and fix everything by myself. I started seeing that I wasn't alone. One important thing I learned during this time was from 2 Corinthians 1:3-4 (NIV): "Praise be to the God and Father of our Lord Jesus Christ, the Father of compassion and the God of all comfort, who comforts us in all our troubles, so that we can comfort those in any trouble with the comfort we ourselves receive from God."

This scripture was echoed by Pastor Martin, who said, "I meet people struggling with devastating news. During those times even the most devout can begin to doubt God's presence. But often what helps them to regain trust is a simple question: 'Has God been with you in difficult times in the past?'"[18] The answer is yes. I believe that's part of why we go through struggles. As the above scripture tells us, we are going through this to see the comfort that the Lord will provide us, so that we will be able to provide the same comfort to others when they are in need.

As I continued my self-examination, another Ryan Stevenson song that truly spoke to me was "All Yours." The lyrics that spoke life into me were about how, when God takes the blindfold off our eyes, it's painful to work through the things we see in

---

18   Martin, James. *Jesus: A Pilgrimage.* New York, NY: HarperOne, 2016.

ourselves. But we eventually find freedom in letting go, because of the foundation of truth and grace He's laid in our lives.

These lyrics are so true; this was what I was going through. Working through and confronting my issues was truly humbling. It caused me to search deep into my heart and see what was not of God. When you start to see the things that are blocking your walk, then you can start to fix them. It is true humility that will bring a man to a place where he sees and acknowledges his errors.

Receiving God's Discipline

I also wrote in my journal about the concept of God punishing or disciplining us. There is a difference between the two, and people often get them confused. In 1 Corinthians 11:31-32 (NIV), the Apostle Paul shows us that the Lord doesn't punish, He disciplines:

> *"But if we were more discerning with regard to ourselves, we would not come under such judgement. Nevertheless, when we are judged in this way by the Lord, we are being disciplined so that we will not be finally condemned with the world."*

A.J. Swoboda said this, "Judgment is a form of grace. In judgment, you may feel rejected, but you are simultaneously being acknowledged as a human being who is loved. By taking time to confront you, God is equally taking time to love you where you are. The Lord disciplines the ones he loves (Hebrews12:6)." [19] This was a big step in my faith, understanding that I was expe-

---

19 Swoboda, A. J. *The Dusty Ones: Why Wandering Deepens Your Faith.* Grand Rapids, MI: Baker Books, 2016.

riencing discipline rather than God punishing me. It was comforting to understand that the love the Lord has for us is one that disciplines through love.

I would tell my players when they made mistakes that I was not punishing *them*; I was punishing their decision. The Lord's discipline is just that. I never placed a correlation on this until now.

As I know today, my old sinful life will always be with me, but as Christ died a slow death for our sins, my death to sin will be slow. And, as Christ was raised, so will I be raised from this to a life of righteousness.

"My old self has been crucified with Christ. It is no longer I who live, but Christ lives in me. So I live in this earthly body by trusting in the Son of God, who loved me and gave himself for me." (Galatians 2:20, NLT)

The cross is a symbol of many things, but an important one is that the cross represents how our old self will die slowly, as Christ did. As we mature in Christ—as we walk in humility and submit to the rule and discipline of the Lord in our life—our old self fades, and the nature of sin fades. We find that we sin less because what we used to do becomes uncomfortable.

Looking back through my journals, trying to decide what I wanted to include in this book, I was able to see objectively my new walk with Christ, and what has taken place in a very short amount of time! I see how God is alive in my life and that He is guiding me through this struggle.

A good friend and client of mine was going through a storm of his own and I prayed for a verse that I could share with him and was led to Deuteronomy 31:6 (NLT): "So be strong and courageous! Do not be afraid and do not panic before them. For the Lord your God will personally go ahead of you. He will neither fail you nor abandon you." This is a verse for all of us to remember when faced with a struggle. This is where faith comes in. We must not fear.

I learned this later when we closed Summit for good, as you will read in the following pages. As Tony Evans wisely said, "If God is taking a long time with you on your detour, it is because he is trying to take you deeper on the inside first. He is trying to develop and strengthen you to sustain the destiny in store, difficult roads, often leads to the most magnificent destinations."[20] When I read this, my thought was, *Then I am going somewhere unbelievable? Because this detour it is taking a long time!*

"Wash me clean from my guilt; purify me from my sin. For I recognize my rebellion; it haunts me day and night." Not sure who said this or where I heard it, but it resonates with me. Guilt and rebellion are two things that will block your faith and growth. We must face our past in order to reach our future.

RELFECTION or DISCUSSION

What has been your biggest struggle in your walk with Jesus?

Do you feel that your life is messier after you met Jesus? Explain your answer.

---

20   Evans, Tony. *Detours: The Unpredictable Path to Your Destiny.* Nashville, TN: B & H Publishing Group, 2017.

How does 2 Corinthians 12:8-10 speak to you?

Chapter Nine

SEEING GOD

"The purpose of the Bible is not to replace God;
the purpose of the Bible is to lead us to God."
~ A.W. Tozer

F our months after "the storm" started, which was a cascade
of difficult situations, one of the struggles ended: we were
finally about to come to an agreement to close our second
fitness center location. However, my brother Jason's wife, Jessica,
was very ill in the hospital, so we were not out of the storm yet.

The business was still struggling. It was a weekly battle to
meet payroll and pay bills. I would pray that the Lord would
provide, and He did. There were times when payroll was the
coming Monday and on Thursday I didn't have the money in the
bank. Then we would get a new client, or some renewals would
come through, and the payroll was covered. In my reading on
May 1st that year, I was reading in Psalms 18:4-6 (NLT):

"The ropes of death entangled me; floods of destruction swept over me. The grave wrapped its ropes around me; death laid a trap in my path. But in my distress I cried out to the Lord; yes, I prayed to my God for help. He heard me from his sanctuary; my cry to him reached his ears."

Seeing this come true, it was easy to start having deeper faith and a willingness to try to walk in the light, abiding in His Word. Through this struggle, one thing happened: my faith increased, and my life was really changing. What I mean by this is that, when you accept Christ, you aren't sure what happens next. Most of us have been a witness to the altar call at the end of a church service, where the pastor asks everyone to close your eyes then continues with asking if there is anyone who would like to accept Christ. Hands are raised and the pastor prays over them, and then . . . what happens? In most of the churches I have been in, those attached to "the hands that were just raised" are invited to stop by a table or booth in the foyer of the church to get some information. Some stop, some don't. Then what happens? Are they the seed that fell on the rocky ground and never takes root? We sometimes never see them again.

What we need to be doing is *discipleship.* We need to connect them with a mature Christian who can answer questions that they will have. If it weren't for my mentors, who were willing to disciple me, I would not be where I am in my walk right now. What I think we as a body should be doing after the altar call is having coffee with those people, talking with them, and making them feel welcome.

Jesus told us He would teach us to be "fishers of men," but there is no clear instruction as to what we are to do after we catch them. So let us start catching and growing; growth can only come when you learn and continue to learn. We need each other to grow, to learn from each other.

"Needing," and being honest about my needs, has been a new thing for me, following closely on the heels of vulnerability. What if "needs"—and I mean needs in and of themselves—are an essential part of the way God has established that humans should live their lives? In other words, needing each other is how God wants us to live. What if God created us to need so that we would have to lean on one another?[21] I think He did. God didn't create us to be alone. Look at the Garden, He even said the man shouldn't be alone!

I believe we need to get back to leaning on one another. With the social media in today's world, we are becoming more and more isolated (it's counterintuitive, I know). We don't even need to leave home to work anymore with Zoom, Skype, and other technologies. Technology is great, but we can't let it separate us from the one thing we were created for: and that's to need one another. So often the way we see God best is through our Christian brothers and sisters.

More Losses

I would soon find out how much I needed the support of my family in Christ. In April of 2015, we lost our oldest brother, Steve. He passed away due to kidney and liver failure. I owe

---

21 Swoboda, A. J. *The Dusty Ones: Why Wandering Deepens Your Faith*. Grand Rapids, MI: Baker Books, 2016.

Steve a lot for what he did for the family when our dad left. I thank God that I had the chance to tell him that before he passed.

Even though Steve didn't accept Christ (he believed in the Big Bang Theory until about a month before he passed), he had the heart of Christ. He would do anything for anyone. If Steve was walking down an aisle in a store and if someone was coming from the other direction, Steve would move and wait for that person to pass before he would continue with what he was doing.

He lived his life caring for our mom. He was one of the gentlest people I knew. When Steve was in the ICU for his last time, he was unconscious, and we didn't know if he would recover or not. I was speaking with my mentor, Scotty, about Steve's faith (or lack thereof). I told Scotty I was worried that Steve was not going to heaven because he had never accepted Christ as his savior (more on this in the next chapter). But this was not all I would have to face.

Not long afterward, in May of 2017, my sister-in-law, Jessica, would lose her battle with addiction and pass away on Mother's Day. Jess was born on her moms' birthday and passed on Mother's Day. I can't imagine how her mom felt. The good news is that her mom was a very strong Jesus person and had great faith in the Father. She and I would have some amazing talks on faith, life, and death. To this day, we chat from time to time just to catch up on what the other is doing and in most of the conversations we end up talking about Christ. I have to say that the sadness of Jess passing was filled with so many things pointing to the evidence of God. And, even after Jason moved in with me, this continued.

Before Jess passed, I arrived at the hospital one day to witness what I would later tell Jason was the picture of unconditional love. That day, I silently watched Jason care for Jess without him knowing I was there. It was an amazing thing, the love that he showed for her. At that moment, I knew that love does show up in everything we do. I wish I could have taken a picture of what I saw because the words I write recalling this do not do it justice. The night Jess passed was one I will never forget. I received the call from the nurse around 3:30 a.m. I stumbled out of bed, threw some clothes on, and headed for Seattle. When I arrived at the hospital, Jess was already home with the Lord.

I saw Jason and asked how he was doing. He replied saying he was okay. He had a peace about him, and he shared the following story with me:

"Bro, I woke up to the nurse giving her medication. We started to chat when he asked how we had met. Jessica LOVED the story, so I told him how she stopped me in my tracks on my first day at the Boeing plant in Renton. She was so beautiful that I literally stopped walking.

When my trainer turned and asked what was up, I responded with, 'Who is THAT?'

He said, 'Oh, that's Jessica; don't bother, she's high maintenance.'

I said back to him, 'I don't care what you say she is, I just want to be her friend so I can be next to her.' She was breathtaking, to say the least!

After I finished the whole story, the nurse told me that if I needed anything, to let him know. He had to tend to other patients. When he left, I got up and went to the restroom. I looked and saw my Jess laying there peacefully, just as beautiful as that moment I first saw her. I walked up to her and leaned over for a kiss on the forehead. I held her hand and told her that she had fought and suffered long enough. I told her that I was well aware of her concerns about me. I let her know that I was moving in with John, and her mom would watch out for me. I told her that I would not go down the wrong path—drugs, I mean. I leaned down and whispered to her, 'It's okay Jess, if you want to go be with Jesus, go. I will be fine. Go rest and I will see you soon.'

As I looked at her, only a few seconds had passed when she took a very labored breath. There was a long pause, then one last breath in, then out, and she was gone. I looked at the clock and it was 2:50 a.m. She took my breath away again. I struggled the entire time I was there with her, (the two weeks, I mean) with the thought, Do I want to be there and watch her take her last breath, or do I want to be asleep when it happens? I didn't want that image burned into my memory forever.

But God knew what He was doing and woke me up so I could tell her those things. We always would tell each other, 'I love you,' and seal it with a kiss before we left each other, even if it was only a quick trip out to the store and back. You never know when it's your time, so we wanted those to be the last words we had heard the other say. I got to do that before she went to heaven.

Bro, they woke her up, two weeks ago, and those were her last words she said to me. John, that's a God-thing."

After listening to Jason's story, I knew that the Lord had His hand all over this. This was a story I would hear Jason repeat to others that day. What a beautiful moment! Seeing the Lord's presence at the darkest times, and placing peace over my brother, was and is truly amazing.

So, in the course of a few years, I lost a lot and was going through a lot. When it was happening, I felt that I was under attack from the enemy. I may have been. But now, looking back on this time from where I am now, I also believe that God used this to strengthen my faith.

I would ask you, when you are in times like these, to remember that Jesus struggled. I believe He modeled this for us so that we would know that to struggle is part of our walk. He even questioned His Father, and we can too. He invites us to question Him. But be prepared for Him to ask you questions, and you might not find your answers; they might be in the mystery box. That is how our faith is built and strengthened.

Building and Exercising Faith

When you are in a situation that you see no way out of, remember the Israelites as they left Egypt and found themselves standing at the Red Sea, with the Egyptian army bearing down on them. I bring this up because this story spoke to me when I was studying in seminary. This is what came to me: When I was reading in Exodus 14 the Lord spoke to me in a very clear voice. I had read this before, but it never spoke to me in this way. (This is what I love about the Bible; you can read the same text at different times in your life, and it will speak to you in a different way or maybe not at all. It is truly the Living Word.)

This particular day, what I heard about the story of the parting of the Red Sea and the Exodus from Egypt was the following, which I wrote in my journal:

"The journey of the Israelites out of Egypt was to show us that from time to time the Lord will place us in situations that look dark, that look frightening, that look like there is no hope—and that our past life was better than what lies ahead of us. With the enemy looming and no escape visible to the Israelites, God provided a path for them, even though their faith was not mature enough to stand without fear.

This was God's will. This was not a test of faith; this was a sign of God's faithfulness to His people. This was to strengthen their faith, to show them and us that no matter how dark, no matter how hopeless their or our situation looks, we need to have faith. Even God will allow the enemy behind us, just as He did in this case, or in front of us as He does later in the Scriptures. We need to know that God will provide us with a way and provide us victory over our enemy or our situation.

When He places us there, it's for His purpose, not ours; we must have faith and know that victory will come. The Lord is using the situation to strengthen our faith, not to hurt us or punish us. Then, when God provides the victory, just as in this story, we must give all the praise and glory to God and sing a new song."

This came to me right before Covid hit us. I share this because when Covid hit, I found myself in another battle: losing Summit Strength & Conditioning, because of Covid. We were going to have to close the doors for good. I wasn't sure what was going to happen or how things were going to unfold. I was standing there with no visible way out. So, what I did was I gave the situation to God.

I prayed daily that He would provide and get me through this, and He did. Even though we would lose a lot, we could have lost more. And He made a way out for us. My faith grew by leaps during this time. I would tell people now that it was a blessing that we closed the gym. The things I saw happen during this time were only because of Him. We were able to get out of our lease early, sell off all our equipment quickly, and I was able to pay back some of those whom I owed some of what they invested. Others forgave what I owed, and I thank them and may God bless them for that.

Watching God work in this was amazing. It is hard to put it into words. All I can say is that we had very few hurdles in selling off everything and negotiating the closure of our lease. Because we had gone through this once before, in closing the Lakewood location, there was no way we could have done what we did in the time we had without help from God. I prayed daily and had faith that it would happen.

Now, I did my part in this. The big lesson I learned is that when you pray, then you have to do your part. You can't just pray, "have faith," and do nothing. You have to do your earthly part and when you do both, that's when you get movement. This was a "GOD THING."

I am not going to say that I haven't had any struggles since this and that I won't have any more, but what I will say is that the struggles are going to be easier to handle and face when I have seen the Lord work in my life, as I have.

"The cross is rough, and it is deadly, but effective. It does not keep its victim hanging there forever. There comes a moment when its work is finished, and the suffering victim dies. After that is resurrection glory and power, and the pain is forgotten for joy that the veil is taken away and we have entered in actual spiritual experience the Presence of the Living God."[22]

During my struggle, there was growth, which is not uncommon. During this time, as I started to go deeper in my study, I found myself asking questions of the Bible. We all do this, but we need to make sure we have the right paths to help us answer these questions. Don't rely on Google! Look in the Bible, speak with mature Christians, look into Mathew Henry's Bible Commentary, then you might find the answer. Don't get discouraged if you don't find the answer though. As Scotty taught me when we don't find the answer it's because it's in the "Mystery Box" as he calls it. When he told me this, I told him, "I didn't like the Mystery Box," but, when you find that your answer is in this box, your faith is being tested and strengthened. One of the first questions I had was: if everyone has a purpose (which I believe we do), then was Judas's purpose to betray Jesus? If that was his purpose, then why did he kill himself? And is he in heaven?

Another is, what happened to Lazarus after he was resurrected? He came out of the grave and was only mentioned once after that. He was said to have been Jesus's best friend so where did he go?

---

22 Tozer, A. W. *The Pursuit of God: The Human Thirst for the Divine.* Chicago: Moody Publishers, 2015.

What I found led me to the following, and this is just my take on these stories. Judas didn't kill Jesus; it was God's plan that Jesus was to be sacrificed for us. He used Judas, the Religious Leaders, Caiaphas, and the others to execute this plan. Judas is most likely not in heaven; for one thing, he didn't seek forgiveness for what he did. Peter, after denying Jesus three times, wept, and sought out forgiveness.

As for Lazarus, the Bible only mentions him one more time after his resurrection, placing him in attendance when Mary was washing Jesus's feet. After that, his whereabouts are just theory. So this is in the mystery box for sure.

Sharing My Faith

I started posting on Facebook what I called "My Daily Bread." It began with a verse from my morning Bible study that spoke to me during that time. My counselor, Christina, knew I was posting this.

One day, Christina prompted me to look at the word "joy." She wanted me to journey through the Bible with the word "joy," so for the next two hundred and forty-three days I posted every verse in the Bible that had joy in it: one hundred and seventy-five in the Old Testament, and sixty-eight in the New Testament. It was a very enlightening experience for me. The reason for this was that Christina wanted me to start seeing the joys around me—even the little ones, such as a sunset, or simply the smell of freshly cut grass. You get the idea. And it worked like most of Christina's homework assignments did. The following is a Facebook post I made during this assignment:

New Year's Resolution

Let's try something this year. Instead of losing weight, eating better, exercising, let's all do something that will change our community, our state, and the world. Let's love deeper. Let's forgive those who have hurt us, and ask for forgiveness from those that we have hurt. Let's try to live each day with the love that Jesus modeled for us. We can have everything, but if we don't have love, we have nothing. This is my resolution for this year. If you agree and are willing to join me, then copy this to your timeline and let's change the world by loving one another.

Love offers life. It softens the dark moments and keeps the heartbeat of hope alive. Love is both a mysterious friend and, at times, a terrible disappointment. Forgiving love is the inconceivable, unexplainable pursuit of the offender by the offended for the sake of a restored relationship with God, self, and others.

-John Jarman

As I came to the end with "joy," I started praying to find the next word. A few days went by and the word "promise" kept coming up. So, "promise" it was, for the next three hundred and sixty-four days. Sometime during this series I surpassed one thousand "Daily Bread" posts. I know this only because I use a hashtag, #4thWatch. I am pretty sure there is no one else using that hashtag and I was making the post one morning and happened to see that #4thWatch had been posted one thousand-plus times. When I saw that, I couldn't believe it had been that many posts.

As I was writing this manuscript, the "promise" series ended and I started my journey with "faith." As of this day, March 9th, 2021, I am nine posts into the five hundred and seven posts I anticipate. I can't wait to see what this will reveal. When I started this, I was doing it for me. But over time, I have had a number of people tell me that they look forward to "My Daily Bread" and that it is encouraging and inspiring to them. (I sometimes misspell a word to see if they are really reading the post and they are. I would do this from time to time when I was coaching to see if the coaches and players were truly paying attention!)

You can find me on Facebook, Instagram, and Twitter if you want to follow "My Daily Bread." I have just recently started adding the Daily Bread to Instagram.

RELFECTION or DISCUSSION

Do you believe that God punishes or disciplines us? Explain your answer.

Has your walk through a storm helped you comfort someone else? How was your faith strengthened by this?

How has your propensity for sin changed over the years as you have grown closer to Christ? (We have ALL sinned so you cannot skip this question by saying you have never sinned.)

Chapter Ten

THE INVISIBLE WAR

"Stay alert! Watch out for your great enemy, the devil.
He prowls around like a roaring lion,
looking for someone to devour."(1 Peter 5:8, NLT)

Forty-three times an evil spirit is mentioned in the Bible. In Genesis, we see that a fallen angel is able to convince Eve to eat from the tree of knowledge. Paul tells us to put on the armor of God, so we can stand against the devil's schemes. Peter tells us that the devil prowls around like a lion, looking to devour someone. So, there is plenty of biblical evidence that a war is taking place. It's not something you will hear that often from the pulpit on Sunday morning. But we need to understand that the war is real, and we have to know how to battle the attacks—not if, but when they happen. This is another reason we need to lean on others.

When I first became a Christian, I didn't know what to do. I didn't even know that it was the devil attacking me. How do we *know* if it's the devil or if it is God testing us? There is a difference, but what is it? It is my belief that when God is testing our faith to strengthen us, there is a way out, or things point to God. We might not see it at first, but as we pray and continue to lean into Jesus, our vision becomes clearer. When the devil is attacking you, nothing makes sense; there is not a clear reason for what is happening, and you cannot see the light. Everything looks dark.

Suiting Up for the Battle

"A final word: Be strong in the Lord and in his mighty power. Put on all of God's armor so that you will be able to stand firm against all strategies of the devil. For we are not fighting against flesh-and-blood enemies, but against evil rulers and authorities of the unseen world, against mighty powers in the dark world, and against evil spirits in the heavenly places." (Ephesians 6:10-12, NLT)

Each of us is engaged in a fight every moment of every day—the spiritual battle between God and Satan for our soul is real. This is a daily battle. We must be on the watch, put on the armor God provides, and engage in the battle using the weapons that God has provided us.

Paul's message in this didn't hit home with me for a long time. What I now believe from this is that, as long as we pray daily as Paul tells us, with all kinds of requests and on all occasions, and develop a true understanding of the Word, we will be mindful of this battle. To face the battle, we MUST understand the Word. Just as Jesus taught us by His example when he faced Satan in the desert after his baptism (see Matthew 4). I have to say that I am far better prepared to face the battle now. Since that day in November, I have been getting up at 4:30 a.m. (the "4th Watch") to pray and read the Word. This practice, along with what I've learned in my mentoring, discipleship, and seminary, has strengthened my faith so I can face the battles that I previously could do nothing about. Within this chapter, it is my hope to softly break the ignorance of the invisible war through my own interface with the invisible world, research, and speaking with others who are in the war themselves.[23]

I believe that we all are in this fight every day, no matter where we come from or where we are in our spiritual walk. I started understanding this more and more after one of my counseling sessions with Christina in 2010, and finding Scotty, and also through the teaching of Rick Warren in his series "The Invisible War: Winning the Battle Within."

Neil Anderson wrote in the foreword to Don Basham's book, *Deliver Us from Evil*, "The Bible clearly exposes the battle between Christ and the Anti-Christ, between the Spirit of truth and the father of lies, between the true prophets and false prophets, and between the Kingdom of God and the kingdom of darkness. Every believer is in this battle, whether he or she likes it or not, and that is why we are all admonished to put on the armor of God, stand firm and resist the evil one." I felt for some time that

---

23   This chapter contains parts of author Neil Anderson's work, Scotty Kessler's, and Don Basham's book, *Deliver Us from Evil.*

I was in a spiritual tug of war for my soul and even expressed this to Christina in our counseling sessions together.

I have been in the Invisible War all my life. I have told people that I was one of Satan's strongest soldiers, and that he wasn't going to let me out of his army without a fight. This is an area of Christianity that many people don't want to believe, and if they do believe, they don't like talking about it or preaching about it from the pulpit. I personally have only heard two pastors talk about this topic in a sermon.

The Ephesians 6 passage I mentioned earlier tells us that we are in a spiritual battle. I have seen the battle manifest physically twice in my life. We need to know Satan's strategies, and we need to know how to use the armor of God to help us have victory in this battle.

Satan will stop at nothing to damage your position and identity in Christ. He can deceive you into believing that you are not acceptable to God and that you'll never amount to anything as a Christian. Then you will live according to those debilitating thoughts rather than in the freedom and wholeness available to you in Christ. You will stay stuck. I know this because that was me. I thought, *I have sinned too much, I have done so many things wrong, I have hurt so many people.* I was stuck, but I see the lies now and I know how to fight. Author Neal Anderson wrote:

What thoughts about yourself maybe deceptions generated by Satan?

That I'm unworthy of love.
That I will also be alone.

That I will never be a good Christian.
That I will never be successful.

God calls you a saint, and that glorious truth should
overshadow
the deceptions about yourself that Satan would have
you believe.
What truths about your identity in Christ can you use
to counter Satan's
deceptions about who you are?

That I am a loved child of God.
That God chose me into his family
That God will never forsake me or abandon me.
-Neil Anderson

I learned to see the lies and then give them to Christ in prayer. It seems simple, but I can tell you from experience that it is not that simple. It takes time and it takes help from mature Christians (and sometimes counselors and mental health professionals) to guide you through.

The Battle Manifests

One day in a session with Christina, we got very close to uncovering the true reason for my depression, shame, and self-destructive lifestyle, and the lack of memory of my childhood. Christina and I were working on memory recovery, and we were trying to unlock the part of my past that I cannot remember. I recently met with her, and we revisited this day.

The session started at around noon, just like most of them. I was sitting on her couch in my normal place with her directly across the room. Christina's office is very comfortable and inviting, overlooking a small, fenced yard, with a desk to the left as you enter her office. Her chair is on the left wall and the couch is just opposite of that. At the end of the couch is a table with a lamp and a box of Kleenex, which I used often during our sessions.

On the wall above her chair are two pictures, one of a wooden bridge that leads into the woods and the other of Chambers Bay (a golf course in University Place, Washington). I would at times stare into these pictures as we talked.

Christina asked me to think back to my earliest memory and, as she tells it, I started speaking very slowly. I don't recall a lot of what happened that day and so the following is what I do recall and what Christina later told me she experienced during our visit to talk about this session.

As I recall, the room felt as if it was shrinking, and the air started to get heavy and "sucked out." She told me that she felt the opposite: it felt as if there was a pressure in the room and a feeling of getting cold. The room felt dark, and, if you recall, my session was at noon so there was plenty of light in her office. As we reflected about this day, we both agree that there was someone in the room with us.

As I sat on the couch and the session progressed, I felt like I was being held down by whatever was in the room with us. I clearly felt two hands on my chest, pushing down. I could feel every finger on both hands. The pressure was so great that I could not get up out of the position I was in. The next thing I recall was hearing Christina's voice, and when I opened my eyes, I saw the fear in her face and heard her say "that she couldn't continue the session for her safety." The demonic presence was real and so evident that Christina had to stop the session.

It was the first time I had ever truly felt a spirit or presence like that. After we stopped, hearing Christina's reaction and what she felt only confirmed what I was feeling. And, as I later sat reflecting with her again, she revealed more to me that only continued to validate that there was a demonic spirit with us that day. She told me that the demon, or whatever was there, let her know that I belonged to him and that, if we didn't stop, he would take her as well. Below are her notes from that session:

Holland Health, PLLC Christina Holland, LMFT Owner, Psychotherapist

It has been several years since the event occurred, although I can clearly remember the experience as if it were yesterday. It's funny how the mind works sometimes. I have been retreating from this topic ever since it happened too. Such a paradox . . . the mind. Having said that, the following is a recounting of my memory of a session between myself and John.

It was early on in our work, which was moving forward well. John was curious about memory gaps in his childhood. I recall telling him I was not an expert at suppressed-memory work, but we agreed to take small, measured steps, to see if it helped him. It was later in the day, and our meeting was getting started with updates and new information. He requested we try to recall the last thing he remembered.

He described being twelve years old and being in his bed when he heard his parents arguing in the kitchen. He recalls sitting up and deciding he wasn't going to let anything bad happen between them. As he continued to tell his story, a strange sensation occurred in the room. John became very still and his voice slowed down in the telling of what happened next.

I experienced a feeling of hackles rising on my neck and a shiver pulled my shoulders up to my ears. The room changed, for the briefest moment, and it was no longer safe. I asked John to stop and raised the tone of my voice to sound firm and loud. And then we both let out big breaths of air and were quiet.

John was able to sit up and readjust his posture and I asked him if he was all right and if he knew what had just happened in the room. He reported feeling as if a heavy pressure was building on his chest, pushing him down, into the couch. I restated my inexperience in this scope of practice and shared my personal concerns about opening up my therapeutic space to anything unsafe in nature. John understood and agreed it was an unpleasant moment and would not pursue memory work at that time.

And yet that session stuck with both of us. We spent several months exploring faith and religion and spiritual mysteries. Working with John drew out my own complicated relationship with God and religion. We both understood I could not be the therapist for the work he was seeking. And, I am very grateful and honored to have been understood.

Thank you, John, for the opportunity to unpack and reflect on our journey. I wish you well, always.

We, I, had a choice to make whether to go there and confront this demon without her or go ahead with our work without ever knowing. This was not an easy choice to make, because I felt I needed to know. Christina didn't want to go with me on this journey and I understand why she was afraid, for her emotional safety and mine as well. She said that she wasn't sure what the outcome of this journey would be. And, because what was waiting for us was so dark, it could potentially do more harm than good.

She continued with saying that there was a reason why I didn't remember this time of my childhood. I didn't want to continue counseling without her because of the trust I had in her. I also didn't want my evil to hurt her. So, I decided to just continue the work without knowing. During a session sometime later, she said she was ready and strong enough to make that journey, but I chose not to put either one of us in that situation. I wasn't sure it would change anything, and the risk seemed too great—if the demon still existed.

Battles Continue

I experienced another personal event that shows the evidence of the Spiritual War when my brother Steve was in the ICU at Virginia Mason Medical Center in Seattle. He had been there for a few days and was unconscious for most of the time he was there. I wasn't sure that he was going to make it through this.

As I mentioned earlier, Steve was not a Christian; he believed in Darwinism. So, I was heading up to the hospital armed with the prayer that Scotty had given me and the knowledge that I might end up facing a demonic power. I entered the room and Steve was still unconscious. We were alone in the room, so I started to pray over him a quiet prayer for him to accept Christ. As I prayed, Steve woke up and looked at me had said, "GET OUT!" in a voice, I have never heard before. It was a dark evil voice.

Steve was a very soft-spoken, meek person. My thought was, *Here I go; Scotty was right.* So, I kept praying, and after a few minutes he awoke again and said, "GET THE #&@% OUT!"

This time it was so loud that the nurse came into the room to see what was going on. I asked her if she was a Jesus person. She said, "Yes."

I continued, "Well, you can stay if you want but I'm not sure what is going to happen. I am praying over my brother, and I am now working against a demonic spirit." She then left the room. I started praying again, and one more time Steve woke up and repeated the same words. Then he was back out.

I continued to pray, and Steve woke up again; this time, however, he looked at me and said, "I need to be saved."

I thought, *WHAT!?* but didn't say that. I said, "Okay, repeat what I say, Steve." Then we prayed the prayer of acceptance together and talked for a couple of hours. The conversation was mostly wrapped around questions Steve had. I don't recall the questions, other than the couple that centered around whether or not he was going to heaven. I told him he would now because he had accepted Christ as his savior. Shortly after that, I left and returned a couple of days later.

As I arrived, Steve was watching TV, he was watching *A.D.: The Bible Continues.* I asked, "What are you watching?"

He replied, "I want to know more."

I said, "Okay, what do you want to know?"

"Am I saved?" he asked.

"Yes, Steve, you are saved," I said. "Do you remember waking up the other day and asking to be saved, and then we said that prayer together?"

"Yes," he replied.

"Then you are saved, my brother. Welcome to the family," I told him. "What else do you want to know?" I asked.

He asked, "How can it be that easy?"

I told him, "God gave His son to purchase our righteousness with His own blood, that even though we have sinned, God sees us as righteous, and we are saved from the punishment we all deserve. The suffering Jesus went through was for us; he paid for our sins."

There were a few more questions and answers, but that was the gist of it. Fast forward, Steve was sent home in hospice care after another hospital visit, and we knew it wouldn't be long before we would lose him. But I felt better knowing he had accepted Christ; I think he felt more at peace as well.

Once we had him home and settled in, we invited some of Steve's co-workers, family, and friends over to Jason's for basically a goodbye celebration. What a treat it was to see those who showed up, and to hear their stories of my brother—stories that made us all laugh, some that made us cry.

After everyone had left, Jason and Jess were cleaning up. Leah and I took Steve for a walk. We put Steve in the wheelchair and headed down the road.

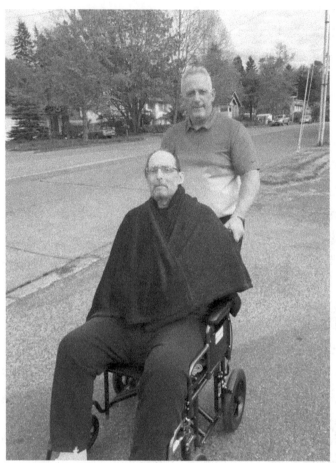

Taking my brother Steve for a walk in his wheelchair

It was a sunny day in Seattle, which made the walk enjoyable. As we walked, I looked over to a park that we were passing, and on the small concrete fence I noticed a book lying on the fence. I walked over toward it and, as I got closer, I could tell it was a Bible. My first thought was, *What is a Bible doing here?* As I reach the Bible and looked down, I saw it was opened to Psalm 51, David's prayer for forgiveness.

I picked it up, placing my fingers in that section so I wouldn't lose the page. I then looked through it, trying to see if it had a name of whom it might belong to. What I found was a list of names, all in Spanish, but it was an English Bible.

I walked back over to where Steve and Leah had stopped, and said, "Steve, look at this, this is a sign, brother, that God wants you to know that you are forgiven. This is the prayer of forgiveness." This was certainly a "GOD THING!" I read the Psalm to him, then I placed the Bible back on the wall where I had found it and we continued our walk. After returning to Jason's, Leah and I shared what had happened with Jason and Jess and they were blown away.

When Leah and I left, I drove back by the park. Something made me want to see if the Bible was still there, and it wasn't— the Bible was gone. Two days later, Steve passed, and by faith I know he is home in our Father's arms.

RELFECTION or DISCUSSION
Have you ever seen evidence of the spiritual war? If yes, explain.

What do you do when you feel attacked by Satan?

Do you have a spiritual mentor? If so who? If not, who could serve as a mentor to you?

Chapter Eleven

UNDERSTANDING THE WAR

"When we ignore evil, whatever it is, we give it more power."
~A.J. Swoboda

When I found Pastor Rick Warren's series "The Invisible War," it not only validated my thoughts, but it provided clarity to what I had experienced for years. You see, when I would start walking with God, my old life would rise up, and then sin, transgression, and iniquity would take over. I truly believe this was because Satan didn't want to lose me as one of his soldiers. It felt like I was not able to make a true conversion to Christ, because I had been a warrior in Satan's army for so long that he didn't want to let me go. And I wasn't using the weapons that God has provided for us to use in this war.

Eric Tinglum, a brother in Christ, said to me the first time we talked about my story, "If you weren't a strong soldier, you wouldn't be worth fighting for." I didn't know about the armor of God at this point of my walk. I didn't read the Bible daily and I didn't pray daily—all of which we need to do to win the battles we will face.

The Invisible War is real. As Chip Ingram says in his book by that title: "There is a supernatural, angelic being who fell from Heaven, who took a third of the angels with him, and his job, his goal, and his strategy are to destroy your life, to murder you— spiritually, emotionally, relationally, and physically. He wants to take you out."[24] I walked hand and hand with that angelic being for years, then I was placed right in the center of the battlefield when I started seeking Christ. When I started developing a relationship with Him, Satan would pull me back by using my former life, temptations, and his number-one strategy, deception, against me. And, due to my lack of spiritual strength, I would be back on the wrong side and would lose the battle, "to terrorize your soul, to render you impotent as a believer, to make you worthless to the cause of Christ, and to make your life one of misery and spiritual defeat."[25]

Never Give Up

I am still fighting the battle, even as I write this. Yes, I admit that I have control to say no and to do the right thing, but, as Romans 7 says, I am not always the boss—sometimes sin is! It's not all the time, of course. It's at the right time, in the right way. It's

---

24 Ingram, Chip. *The Invisible War: What Every Believer Needs to Know about Satan, Demons, and Spiritual Warfare.* Grand Rapids, MI: Baker Publishing, 2006, 2015.

25 https://livingontheedge.org/broadcast/spiritual-warfare-101-what-is-the-invisible-war/

when you're low. It's when you're tired. It's when you're traveling. It's late at night. It's after everyone goes to bed. It's when something pops up on the computer screen, and you think . . .

This is when he attacks.

Generational sin, and the fact that I was a victim of human-inflicted evil and didn't seek help for years, added to my sinful nature. My habitual sin, as James McDonald says, "allowed Satan in," and I was left bound. I truly didn't understand the battle until I met and started working with my mentor, Scotty Kessler. This is when I truly understood that there is a battle, and I am right in the middle.

During my time with Christina and Scotty, I read a number of books that were helpful. One of the books that helped me understand the true meaning of evil, and the presence of evil in the world, was a book that Christina had me read as we were trying to uncover what had happened to me as a child, *Trauma and Evil: Healing the Wounded Soul*, by J. Jeffrey Means and Mary Ann Nelson. This book showed me the types of evil and their effect on us as humans.

If you are a victim of any evil, I would suggest you read this book. The reason I suggest it is because, as the author states in his introduction, "The professional perspective from which we come at this task is that of pastoral counseling and psychotherapy. This means we are committed to integrating contemporary theories of psychotherapy and human development with resources offered by Christian faith and theology." This book helped me understand that I was a victim, that evil is truly a force, and that we as Christian sometimes don't admit that there is a true evil at work, or that any of us can fall victim to it.

The other book is *Deliver Us from Evil: A Pastor's Reluctant Encounters with the Powers of Darkness,* by Don Basham. As the cover copy describes, "In this book, Pastor Basham talks about his journey from disbelief to acceptance in the existence of demonic spirits. He talks about the difference between infestation and possession, and how to engage in spiritual warfare. He also describes the biblical tools that bring deliverance from demonic influence."

In an interview with Scotty, I uncovered the following: in this battle, as it says in Ephesians 6:10-12 (NLT):

> ". . . we are not fighting against flesh-and-blood enemies, but against evil rulers and authorities of the unseen world, against mighty powers in the dark world, and against evil spirits in the heavenly places. The battle is against the devil and his cadre of fallen angles. There is no way to determine whether it is a spiritual, emotional battle or if it is a demonic angel involved. But the entry point of this warfare is sin, however. There is no clear way to determine or to know when it has moved from a battle in someone's spirit/soul and moved on to a battle that involves demonic forces, but there will be a strong link to sin. It might be our sins that we initiated, or it may be a response to being sinned against. Then we respond and that's what we are held accountable for; that's where the stronghold can develop. This could be as simple as just grumbling or complaining, or a sin against a person."

Lastly, generational sin can be the link. There is a lot of disagreement in the Body of Christ with regard to this in the new covenant. It's alluded to, in the Bible, in John 9:3. Jesus did seem to reference generational sin in this verse, but this would indicate that we can be held accountable for the sins of our father. For example, a son who grows up in a family of violence can become violent, or one who experiences his parents' divorce will be divorced. Is this simply a learned behavior or is it spiritual in nature? This is where the disagreement lies, and the mystery is: what can we do to be effective in this battle?

We must have certain fundamentals in place to be effective in this battle. For one, we want to try to walk uprightly and be blameless and pure. "Blameless and pure" has to do with a position, and the position has to do with being in right standing with God, and that comes from confession and repentance. We need to walk in a state of acknowledgment or confession of our depravity in general, so it keeps us humble.

In terms of specific known and unknown sins, it's important to be asking forgiveness from God continually—not out of fear that we are going to forget something but wanting to have a right heart and relationship where all the power and all the fruit are accessible. We must pray continually, and have a vertical and horizontal relationship, with both God and man. We must know that the weapons are there and retain our access to them by being in right standing and knowing how to use the weapons God has given us to fight this battle. Then we need to learn how to use them more and more effectively as we mature in our relationship

Repentance Is a Weapon

The enemy will come at us with lies and accusations against our purpose and worth. He attacks us because we don't know our identity in Christ, in order to get us discouraged, depressed, hopeless, tired, broken, and walking in our past sin. When we are walking in the Spirit, with His fruit and power, then we can resist the devil (James 4:7). This is a mental battle. The devil uses deception and lies to disarm us. He cannot take our salvation, but he can deceive us, discourage us, and distract us from the work that God has called us to do.

We have to fight back, and one of the most fundamental ways we do this is through repentance, which is critical to access the weapons of our warfare (see 2 Corinthians 10:3-5) and the armor of God (see Ephesians 6:10-12). Some say that we don't need to repent and confess anymore because we have done it once. This is a crazy lie and a scheme of the devil to keep us from accessing purity and blamelessness, in order to walk in a way that can defeat the devil—not only in ourselves but helping others so that we can fight for others.

Repentance is one of God's greatest gifts to mankind. It brings refreshment and cleansing, wipes away our sin, releases God's compassion toward us, and secures God's forgiveness, and releases the work of His Holy Spirit in us (Proverbs 28:13; Isaiah 44:22; Acts 2:38, 3:19-20). When we walk in repentance and humility, it positions us to walk in our authority in Jesus and resist the devil. When we are walking in our authority, we have no need to fear the devil! Of course, one should be wise to respect an enemy; the Bible says not to be "unaware of his schemes" (2 Corinthians 2:11). Being unaware of the devil's schemes would be ignorance. But we are not to fear him, we are to fear God, and if we fear God we will do a better job of fearing less, becoming fearless. As Paul told Timothy, "For the Spirit God gave us does not make us timid, but gives us power, love, and self-discipline." That word "timid" is part of the root of "intimidation'; in other words, with God's

Spirit in us, we don't need to be intimidated by our enemy. Instead, we can operate in the power of the Holy Spirit!

Fighting the Battle

Within this battle, we need to understand that our will cannot be taken over. The mind, the body, and emotions can be, but we need to understand that the *will* cannot be taken over. As the late Derek Prince said, "The word which is translated in English 'possessed' in the original Greek simply means 'to have a demon.' 'Affected' by a demon is closer to it. 'Possessed' implies ownership, as if the spirit controlled the entire person, which is a much stronger idea than the Greek implies."

People in need of deliverance have some problems that they have not been able to surmount by other means. They may be suffering some form of mental anguish, or some inflaming physical appetite, but they are not "possessed" by it. In fact, in other ways they may by exceptionally strong individuals.

In order to fight this kind of battle, we must become blameless and pure, by confession of sin (i.e., repentance), and, when you are in right standing, then you can begin to clean the house. Now this could be a prolonged battle, depending on how long it's been there. And, as for how strong it is, we find this out when we start to fight, and we see the resistance. Here are some steps to follow that will keep us strong in the fight:

1. **Live by the Scriptures.**
   The Word of God proclaims Satan's defeat. By standing on God's Word, a person who has been delivered can block Satan's attempt to return. Jesus Himself, during

His temptations, withstood Satan by reliance on the written word. "It is written..." he said in response to every allurement of the devil (see Matthew 4). The Scriptures confirm that health, protection, and deliverance are all part of our inheritance in Christ. But we cannot claim these promises if we are not aware of them—and this means prayerful and expectant daily bible reading.

2. **Learn to praise God continually.**

"The devil never has much luck with a grateful man." This apt saying points out that an attitude of thanksgiving and praise can thwart Satan's efforts to dislodge us from our place in Christ. Such an attitude is especially important after deliverance: it is one of the ways we rebuild the walls. "Rejoice evermore," Paul wrote to the Thessalonians, and "in everything give thanks: for this is the will of God in Christ Jesus concerning you" (1 Thessalonians 5:16, 18, KJV).

3. **Protect and guard your thought life.**

The mind is Satan's primary target. By suggestion and insinuation, his temptations subtly begin. Therefore, we must "put on the helmet of salvation" to cover and protect the mind. This means nipping certain conversations in the bud; it means avoiding certain films, books, and environments that we know spell danger for us. It is no sin to be tempted, but to invite and entertain temptation is to hold open a door to the enemy.

4. **Cultivate right relationships.**

Hatred and resentment toward others create the ideal climate for demonic invasion. Just as a person can scarcely be delivered without forgiving those who have injured him, neither can he keep his deliverance for long if he permits bitterness and resentment to creep back in. Maintaining loving relationships with others and practicing continual on-the-spot forgiveness are two of the surest wall builders.

5. **Submit to discipline.**
Demonic problems are often the result of overindulgence of some appetite or weakness of the flesh. For the one delivered, discipline becomes an essential part of keeping the victory—not just self-discipline but also submission to others more mature in Jesus Christ. This means becoming part of a regularly meeting body of Christians and submitting our plans and desires to the wisdom of the group.

You may think I am crazy, or perhaps simply making this up, but the following account actually happened. You likely know Scripture clearly gives several examples of people who were afflicted by "evil" or "unclean" spirits, and we are instructed to guard against this:

"When an evil spirit leaves a person, it goes into the desert, seeking rest but finding none. Then it says, "I will return to the person I came from." So, it returns and finds its former home empty, swept, and in order. Then the spirit finds seven other spirits more evil than itself, and they all enter the person and live there. And so that person is worse off than before. That will be the experience of this evil generation." (Matthew 12:43-45, NLT)

For years, I would wake up around 3:30 or 4:00 a.m. I couldn't understand why this was happening. In talking with Scotty, he said he thought that the Lord was trying to tell me something. He continued by telling me that this was the most spiritual and demonic time of the day. I then began to look into this and started to use this time for prayer and Bible study.

The 4th Watch

When the Romans occupied the Holy Land, they brought their clock with them, which was broken down into four watches, the "fourth watch" being from 3:00 a.m. to 6:00 a.m. In my research, I found that a lot of the most significant events in the Bible happened during the fourth watch: the parting of the Red Sea, Jesus' walking on the water, and His trial started during this watch. It is the most spiritual and demonic time of the day.

I am living proof of this. I gave up control of my life truly during the fourth watch, my addiction occurred in the fourth watch, and now my prayer and Bible study is in the fourth watch. It has been truly amazing to watch what has happened in my life since I have been praying and reading in the fourth watch. I would tell people that I get up at 4:30 a.m. to pray and study, and they would then ask me how I make it through the day. My response was, "I give Him the time in the morning, and He gives me the strength to make it through the day."

I say to Christians, if you believe in Christ, then you have to believe in the evil spirits as well; you cannot have one without the other. I understand the Church not wanting to focus on what I call the "dark side," but it's needed. It's there; it's real. I believe we should teach on this subject more, so, as Christians, we are better prepared for it when it hits.

I was working with Scotty on my own strongholds from my past. What this entailed was daily prayers to attempt to get movement in the spiritual world, to break the chains that had been holding me for years. There was a six-month period of reading and adjusting the prayers based on the movement I was getting while I was reading the prayers.

I am not saying that everyone needs prayer plans like I had. But if you feel that you are being held back by something, then you should seek counsel within your church. My work with Scotty, and my work with Christina, is the only way I became free. A.J. Swoboda said the following in his book *After Doubt*, "Part of loving God is knowing ourselves as God's handiwork."[26] I can say without a doubt at this time in my life I didn't know myself as God's handiwork. I, like a lot of people, felt I was too sinful for God to love me. That thought didn't change until after I got to know myself.

When I read the following, my feelings of pain came flooding back:

> *"The road to recovery requires learning to tell the truth, even if that truth is brutally painful. I'd never been able to tell anyone what was going on inside.*[27]
> *"So, I forced these images back, away, for years, I began [however] to reintegrate that split-off part of*

---

26 Swoboda, A. J. *After Doubt: How to Question Your Faith without Losing It.* Brazos Press, a division of Baker Publishing Group, 2021.

27 Ibid.

*my experience . . . Then, out came this overwhelming
sadness and healing. Integrating the feelings of sadness, rage, or all of the above without action should
be standard operating procedure for all soldiers who
have killed face-to-face. It requires no sophisticated
psychological training.* "[28]

This is what happened to me. I forced everything inside; vulnerability was one of the biggest emotions Christina worked on
with me. I would not tell anyone what was going on, as I have
stated. I would not let anyone in. I did not know what vulnerability was. I do now! I was never taught what it was nor was
it ever modeled for me. The only person I was truly vulnerable
with was Christina. What changed in me to let me be this vulnerable? It's a "GOD THING"! Through everything, God has
softened my heart and changed my image of myself. He took a
heart that was once stone and softened it. I now know what love
and vulnerability are.

Take Heart—Christ Has Already Won
In closing this chapter, I hope I have shed light for you on this
topic of the invisible war. It is real, and everyone is in it whether
we want to be or not. We do have victory through Christ Jesus
and we must stand firm on the Word of God to keep our victory. In doing this, we need to remain humble and remember
what Jesus said in Luke 10:19-20 (NIV): "I have given you the
authority to trample on snakes and scorpions and to overcome

---

28   Marlantes, Karl. *What It Is Like to Go to War.* New York:, NY Atlantic Monthly
     Press, 2011.

all the power of the enemy; nothing will harm you. However, do not rejoice that the spirits submit to you, but rejoice that your names are written in heaven."

The Spirit of God brings us to life spiritually, yet we live in these bodies of flesh that still have a sinful nature. Thus, the battle rages in the lives of believers but, through Christ, the victory is assured!

RELFECTION or DISCUSSION
What are your beliefs on the Invisible War? Have they been challenged by anything in my story?

Have you ever experienced the Fourth Watch?

What are your greatest areas of struggle or "strongholds"? List them here.

Pray now and ask God to show you what you are holding on to. List what you feel He is showing you.

Chapter Twelve

THE NEW

"New doesn't mean perfect. New means that all the building blocks forsomething beautiful are now there."
~ A.J. Swoboda

"The world has yet to see what God can do with a man who is fully yielded to him. And I intend to be that man. It isn't about the mistakes I made. It isn't about the things I regret. It's about the rest of my life doing the will of God."
~ Dale Moody

There came a time in my walk that I did just that: I finally yielded to Him. I finally learned how to give up the past and not let it rule me. My regret, shame, and guilt were gone. Trust me when I say that they still come around at times. However, I am now able to give it to God and move on. Yes, I still make mistakes; we all do. But as I have said, there are fewer and fewer mistakes. I am still not where I need to be. I am a work in progress, just as you are.

I was baptized again when I was with Leah. Scotty helped me set it up. This was what they call an immersion (i.e., submersion) baptism. Eric Tinglum performed the baptism and we used an indoor pool of a friend of Scotty's. I wanted to do this so that I could experience what A.J. calls the two sides of baptism: "the falling into the water and the death, and the raising out of the water into life. Only one of those two can be done on your own, the falling into the water part. The second, of course, is rather difficult to pull off on your own. Baptism is the acknowledgment that you can die on your own, but you must have someone else bring you out of the water."[29] What a beautiful description of baptism—the outward sign that you are born again, and we cannot be born again without the help of Jesus.

Leah and I were still together and committed to trying to make it work even though there were struggles. Things were going great, with the exception of her family not accepting me. Even as you start anew, there are struggles, and sometimes God doesn't answer the prayers that you are praying. This is because He knows where we are going and what we need.

Counseling and weekly meetings with Scotty continued. I even entered Scotty's discipleship class. I had no idea of how to disciple someone. What I learned was a very systematic way to do this that made it very easy and simple to do. Scotty was discipled by Dr. Robert Coleman, who was one of the original Navigators,

---

29 Swoboda, A. J. *Messy: God Likes It That Way.* Grand Rapids, MI: Kregel Publications, 2012.

and the author of a number of books on discipleship and evangelism, including *The Master Plan of Evangelism*. The system Scotty taught me is easy, but the process is not. It takes focus, dedication, and commitment to follow this system that Scotty had developed over the year of his ministry. This was the very first time that I would go this deep into the Word until seminary.

The class met once a week and, in it, we learned "The Big 10." What is the Big 10? The Big 10 is a ten-step guide to disciple new believers and others, to strengthen their relationship with God, understand how to pray, read the Bible, memorize Scripture, prepare a three-minute testimony, and make a gospel presentation and invitation.

No one ever told me that following Jesus would be this much work. But, as in any relationship, it takes commitment. I would have the pleasure of going through Scotty's training twice: once when he taught the men of Life Center, and once during seminary. With his permission, I'm going to share the highlights of that training here.

After you read through the following pages, you will hold the key to true discipleship. If you use the system, you will be able to start disciplining immediately. Remember, this is one of the greatest commandments: "Go and make disciples of all nations" (Matthew 28: 16-20).

"Being a disciple of Christ involved far more than a joyful acceptance of the Messianic promise: it meant the surrender of one's whole life to the Master in absolute submission to his sovereignty."
- Robert Coleman, *The Master Plan of Evangelism*

The Big 10

The following is just an outline, and then I will go into detail. The procedure and documents that follow are reprinted under the permission of Scotty Kessler.

1. Prayer – TACOS
2. Bible Reading (developing some kind of individualized reading plan
3. Bible Memorization ("AWCFROGROL" verses)
4. Learn to Study the Bible (using the NIV Study Bible "helps")
5. The Bible Song (tool to learn the books of the Bible in successive order)
6. The Five Questions (asked regularly/weekly)
7. Review Accountability Questions (recommended at least bi-monthly)
8. Develop Your Testimony (write out a three-minute testimony)
9. Give a Gospel Presentation (based on the AWCFROG-ROL sequence)
10. Give a Gospel Invitation (based on the AWCFROGROL sequence)

These steps are not done in any order. They are done in conjunction with others; step one is teaching your disciple how to pray.

1. **TACOS**

   Scotty uses what he calls "TACOS Prayers"— this is a system to help those who don't pray, or don't know how to pray, with a simple and effective way to pray. You spend approximately one minute in each topic:

   Thanksgiving

   Adoration

   Confession

   Others

   Self

   If you are leading a group, you first ask for members to pray. Then you start the prayer. Then you have the members pray with someone, starting with Thanksgiving, and then the next person starts with Adoration and so on until Self is complete. Then you as the lead close the prayer.

   If you are praying by yourself, you can use the outline to guide you as you talk with God on these topics.

2. **Bible Reading**

   As the leader, you should have a reading plan set up before your first meeting with your group or disciple. One of the best starting places is the book of Matthew. When you are reading with your group, read in the following way: you start reading the first verse then move around the room having each person read one verse then move to the next person. Reading should be about three to four chapters a meeting. You should also provide them with a reading plan for the week until your next meeting.

3. **Bible Memorization**

A - ADMIT (Romans 3:23) – "For all have sinned and fall short of the glory of God."

W - WAGES (Romans 6:23) – "For the wages of sin is death, but the gift of God is eternal life in Christ Jesus our Lord."

C – CONFESS (Romans 10:9) – "That if you confess with your mouth, 'Jesus is Lord,' and believe in your heart that God raised him from the dead, you will be saved."

F - FORGIVE (1 John 1:9) – "If we confess our sins, he is faithful and just and will forgive us our sins and purify us from all unrighteousness."

R - REPENT (Acts 3:19) – "Repent, then, and turn to God, so that your sins may be wiped out, that times of refreshing may come from the Lord."

O - OPEN (Revelation 3:20) – "Here I am, I stand at the door and knock. If anyone hears my voice and opens the door I will come in and eat with him and he with me."

G - GRACE (Ephesians 2:8-9) – "For it is by grace that you have been saved through faith, and this is not from yourselves, it is the gift of God, not by works, so that no one can boast."

R - RECEIVE (John 1:12) – "Yet to all who received him, to those who believed in his name, he gave the right to become children of God."

O - OBEY (1 John 2:3-4) – "We know that we have come to know him if we obey his commands. The man who

says, 'I know him,' but does not do what he commands
is a liar, and the truth is not in him.'"
L - LOVE (John 14:21) – "Whoever has my commands
and obeys them, he is the one who loves me. He who
loves me will be loved by my father, and I too will love
him and show myself to him."

4. **Learn to Study the Bible**
   As the leader, you need to teach your group how to use
   a study Bible. The key is to find one that has cross references that will help you gain context and understanding
   of the passages you are reading, and that will give you
   direction for further study.

5. **The Bible Song**
   For me, "The Bible Song" (a tool to learn the books of
   the Bible in successive order) worked great. The lyrics
   below are to the theme from *Gilligan's Island*. If you
   know *Gilligan's Island*, then you can sing the song:
   BIBLE SONG Lyrics:
   Genesis, Exodus, Leviticus, Numbers, Deuteronomy
   Joshua, Judges, Ruth AND First AND Second Samuel
   First AND Second Kings AND First AND Second
     Chronicles
   Ezra, Nehemiah, Esther, Job, AND THEN THE BOOK
     OF Psalms
   Proverbs, Ecclesiastes, Song of Solomon
   Isaiah, Jeremiah, Lamentations, Ezekiel, Daniel,
     Ho-se-a
   Joel, Amos, Obadiah, Jonah, Micah, Nahum, Habakkuk
   Zephaniah, Haggai, Zechariah, Malachi

Matthew, Mark, Luke, Joh-ohnn, Acts, Romans, Corinthians

Galatians, Ephesians, Philippians, Colossians, Thessalonians

Timothy, Titus, AND Philemon, Hebrews, AND THEN
James

Peter, John, Jude, Revelation—THIS CONCLUDES
OUR SONG

6. **The Five Questions (Asked Regularly/Weekly)**

a) Whom are you praying for to accept Jesus and what
specifically did you do this week to interact with them?

b) Whom are you currently discipling and what specifically did you do this week to equip them in Jesus with
the Big 10?

c) Who are future discipleship prospects and what specifically did you do this week to interact with them?

d) Who are your current mentors and what specifically
did you learn in your interaction with them this week?

e) Who are potential future mentors and what specifically are you hoping to learn in your interactions with
them?

7. **Review Accountability Questions (Recommended at
Least Bi-monthly)**

Develop your testimony—write out a three-minute testimony that entails:

a) Who you were before you gave your life to Jesus.

b) Describe your "life change" circumstances (an actual
"event" or process of weeks/months)\

c) Who you are now, "post-conversion."

8. **Develop Your Testimony**

   Help the disciples in your group write a three-to-five-minute testimony that they will practice in front of the group.

9. **Give a Gospel Presentation (Based on the AWCFRO-GROL sequence)**

   What this means is that you are to use the verses to present the gospel. For example, all fall short, we are sinners, if we confess our sin we are saved, he will forgive these sins, if we repent and turn to God, our sins are wiped out, we must be open to hear his word, we are saved by grace not by our doing, we are children of God, to know him is to obey his word, he will love us.

10. **Give a Gospel Invitation (Based on the AWCFROG-ROL sequence)**

    This is taking a new believer through the verse by having them repeat after you as you lead them through AXC-FROGROL"

"I am a sinner; the wages of sin is death. I confess my sins, and by confessing I am forgiven of my sins. If I repent for my sins and accept the Lord as my savior, my sins will be wiped out. I open my heart and mind to His Word. I am saved by grace, not by what I do. I am now a child of God. I will obey His Word, and I am loved by the Lord."

You can see that the system is not complicated but working through it is; it takes time and effort on your part and your disciple's part. The best part of this is you don't

have to be a Christian for years to disciple: you, yourself, can start to disciple within weeks of starting this
program, and it is encouraging that your disciples start
disciplining soon also.

Other good discipling resources are *Born to Reproduce*, by
Dawson Trotman (Navigators), and *The Master Plan of Evangelism*, by Robert Coleman, which I mentioned earlier.

Going Deeper

As I continued to work with Christina and Scotty to release the
strongholds and to better understand my past and the effect it
had on me, the Spirit led me to wanting to know and to go deeper
into the Word. The only way I knew of doing this was to go to
school. So, meeting with Scotty, I told him that this was what I
felt was being placed on my heart by the Lord, and he agreed. I
will pause here to say, you hear of people saying that God or the
Spirit speaks to them. After a few conversations and praying on
this, I enrolled in Faith Seminary in Tacoma.

Now I have to resay this: I was not an Old Testament reader.
Up until seminary, I never studied the Old Testament. And what
does He do? He places me in Old Testament Review in my first
semester of school. Now that is a "God Thing."

So, looking at the heart of the Old Testament, the Penta-
teuch forced me to face my fears, apprehensions, and miscon-
ceptions about the Old Testament—or, as I used to call it, "The
Dark Side." As the class progressed, my perspective changed,
and I started to see the connection between the Old and New
Testaments. In one assignment, I had to write a paper on an

Old Testament character. I chose Jacob. I found the story of Jacob interesting because he wrestled with God; in some way, I believe we all wrestle with God. As our faith deepens, I think we wrestle more.

RELFECTION or DISCUSSION
Will you use the Big 10 to start a discipleship group? Why or why not?

How many Bible verses have you memorized, if any? Which are your favorites?

What technique do you use? Please share with the group.

What does your prayer life look like? Please share with the group any techniques or models that have been helpful to you. Or, if you would like to grow in your prayer life, ask the group for some of their most meaningful or helpful practices.

Chapter Thirteen

CLEAR VISION

Moses said to the people, "Do not be afraid, God has come to test you so that the fear of God will be with you to keep you from sinning." (Exodus 20:20)

Back to my story.
My brother moved in with me after losing his wife to kidney failure. They were together for over twenty years. I wish I could say it was a good life, but for them, their life was one of addiction. I won't go into all the details, but it was bad. I moved him in with me because I felt if I didn't, he would overdose within a month. I had started seminary and I was in my second semester.

When Jason moved in, he asked one day what I was doing up so early. I told him, and, surprisingly, he started joining me for my 4thWatch prayer and Bible study, which I was very happy about. When this happened, I put the disciple training Scotty had taught me into action. We started our study in the book of Matthew (which, as I said earlier, I believe is the best place to start). When we read together, we read with us switching back and forth on the reading duties, verse by verse, just as Scotty had shown me to do in his disciple classes. Our morning routine was first TACOS prayer; then we would read alternating verses.

Fast forward a few months. We finished The Book of Revelation and Jason looked at me and asked, "Now where do we go?"

I said, "To the beginning; we are going to Genesis." I told you that, before seminary, I was not an Old Testament reader. That is why I started Jason off in Matthew. I felt that Jason would feel the same. But, after having Old Testament Review as one of my first classes in seminary I felt I could answer the questions that Jason might have as we went to "the dark side."

As we got to Exodus, we were reading in chapter 20 one morning and, when it was my turn to read, we were on Exodus 20:20. I read it, and something hit me, but I let it go for the time being. Later that day, I went back to it and read it over and over, meditating on it for a day. Then, it hit me: God's message to me was that this is the clear vision of what God wants us to understand, just like 20/20 is clear vision when we visit the eye doctor. So, the clear vision is, "Moses said to the people, 'Do not be afraid, God has come to test you, so that the fear of God will be with you to keep you from sinning' (Exodus 20:20, NIV).

Later that same day, I started thinking, *How many verses have this address?* So, I went searching. Exodus 20:20 is the first 20:20, and there are sixteen more: twelve in the Old Testament, and four in the New Testament. Ten of them have instructions as to how we are to act and behave as Christians. Here are the sixteen others; the asterisk indicates the ten verses that have instructions:

Leviticus*, Numbers, Deuteronomy*, Judges, 1 and 2 Samuel, 1 and 2 Kings, 2 Chronicles*, Job*, Proverbs*, Ezekiel* Matthew*, Luke, John*, Acts*

This spoke to me so much that I now have this verse tattooed on my right forearm. I spent four and a half years in the Marines and didn't get a tattoo, but now I was getting my first. I had to leave off the first part of the verse to make it fit on my arm ("So Moses said to the people" is not part of the tattoo). This tattoo starts a lot of conversations, and I must admit I love sharing this story. In sharing this, I hope that those people who inquire about it—including you—go and look at these verses to understand God's vision.

Now, running both the golf club's center and my own at Summit, I could not see how I could do the work to maintain good grades in school, so I left seminary. I do plan to return one day to finish.

Christ in Me

As I was writing this, I was hit with a thought about the part of this verse, "God has come to test you." God does test us. The tests are to deepen our faith and make us lean into Him and trust Him more. So, I did another Bible search, looking at all the verses that have the word "test" in them. There are only 35, 21 in the Old Testament, and fourteen in the New Testament, that speak to a true test; here are a few:

"But he knows where I am going. And when he tests me, I will come out as pure as gold." (Job 23:10, NLT)

"Do not listen to them. The Lord is testing you to see if you truly love him with all your heart and soul." (Deuteronomy 13:3, NLT)

"Don't be afraid of what you are about to suffer. The devil will throw some of you into prison to test you. You will suffer for ten days. But if you remain faithful even when facing death, I will give you the crown of life." (Revelation 2:10, NLT)

I would like to think that I have passed the test so far. I have had a few, and I know that my faith has become deeper because of them. So, be ready for your test; it's coming because He wants to know (and wants you to see for yourself) if you love Him. Stay faithful during the test and you will be rewarded.

This brings me back to Leah. Three years after we broke up, I received an Instant Message through Facebook from Leah's mother, Linda, with her permission, I have included her message, because of the reassuring faith message in it:

John,

This has been a long time coming! As a mother, you never quit feeling the need to protect your children. When Leah's husband lied and walked out on his

family, we were one bunch of broken people. I want to apologize for treating you like I did. I know I asked you if you would still go to church if you and Leah didn't work out. You told me yes! I want you to know how you continued your walk with the Lord has been very impressive. You also have had some really tough times and I continue to pray for you and your brother. Life is not an easy journey but with Christ, all things are possible. I ask you to forgive me and may God bless you richly. Once again I am sorry.
In Christ's most precious love,
Linda

I have forgiven you, Linda! Just as I have the rest of the family. I pray for all of you daily. I am also including my reply to Linda:

Linda,

Let me start by saying thank you, and I forgive you in name of Christ our Lord. I would ask you for forgiveness as well. We are all broken and fallen people and I'm just sorry that I wasn't strong enough in my walk to be more Godly.

The Lord has taught me so much over these past months and years. I can truly say that my faith rests in who I am in Christ. And I know and understand that God's work of atonement changes sinners to saints. The radical change, regeneration, is effected at the moment of salvation. The ongoing change in the believer's daily walk continues throughout life. The progressive work of sanctification, however, is only fully effective when the radical, inner transformation by regeneration is realized and appropriated by faith. I want you to know that I have not let one day go by that I have not prayed for Leah, her kids, and you.

Thank you again for your note; it truly touched and humbled me.

Peace to you and with faith from God the Father and the Lord Jesus Christ,

John

That season of life was one of my greatest tests. One of the things I pray for is for people to see Christ in me, and I think that Linda has seen that. It's humbling to know that I have changed enough for someone to see a new part of me. I hope that this shows you that through daily reading and praying with a community you will grow in Christ, and you will be changed from the inside out, and even when you don't know it, you will have become a light of Christ.

The Bible is a living Word. I used to hear that and not understand what they were saying, but I now truly get the meaning of that. I once told someone that what I love about the Bible is that whatever you are going through, when you pick up the Bible, *it will speak to you.* As A.W. Tozer said in his book *The Pursuit of God,* "Come at once to the open Bible expecting it to speak to you. Do not come with the notion that it is a thing which you may push around at your convenience.

It is more than a thing, it is a voice, a word, the very Word of the Living God."

One thing I have learned in this crazy walk with God was said perfectly by philosopher Blaise Pascal, "I have discovered that all the unhappiness of men arises from one single fact, that they are unable to stay quietly in their own room." This took me a long time to be able to do. I now can sit quietly in my own room. This only happened through prayer and learning how to accept me for me and love me for me. You have to love yourself before you can love others. To love you have to understand love. Once I truly saw the love of our Father, I was able to start loving myself.

Picking Up When We Stumble

As I grew, I would still stumble and I would see some of the Christians, those I leaned on and learned from, also fall due to their sinful nature. I would have to work through this because the falls caused me to question my faith and the Church. As I have learned, this is a normal part of our walk. A.J. Swoboda calls this "deconstruction": moments of our walk where we doubt. The question is, *What do we do in those moments?* We are never far from a fall. It is human nature.

We only have two choices when we doubt: one is to go deeper in, or we walk away. I think this is one of the hardest things to deal with in our walk. As Christians, we need others to grow; what we have to guard against is placing them above God. If we idolize them, then when they fall, it can be devastating to our faith. We must place God above all.

The next challenge that I faced was Jason's fall. After three years together and right after Covid hit us, he ended up in a very low place and depressed. It got out of control and, as I tried to get him help, it became a battle. The mental health system in Washington is bad. There is a lack of beds and facilities due to the lack of funding. In addition, the RCW's are very gray as to involuntary detainment.

After a number of attempts to get Jason detained, I started researching the laws and the system. This would lead me to find NAMI, the National Alliance on Mental Illness. I started working with the Pierce County chapter. NAMI works to try to remove the stigma of mental illness, bring awareness, and lobby for better laws.

I believe we must work to remove the stigma of this silent killer. Here is a poem I stumbled across that speaks to the damaging effects of drug and alcohol abuse. I am including it in hopes that it speaks to someone and helps them overcome their addiction.

> *"Hello, my name is DRUGS, or you can call me ALCOHOL, if you like—your choice.*
>
> *I destroy homes, tear families apart, take your children, and that's just the start. I'm more costly than diamonds, more costly than gold, and the sorrow I bring is a sight to behold. And, if you need me, remember I'm easily found. I live all around you, in schools and in town. I live with the rich, I live with the poor, I live down the street, and maybe next door.*
>
> *My power is awesome—*
>
> *try me, you'll see. But if you do, you may never break free. Just try me once and I might let you go, but*

try me twice, and I'll own your soul. When I possess you, you'll steal, and you'll lie. You do what you have to just to get high. The crimes you'll commit, for my narcotic charms, will be worth the pleasure you'll feel in my arms.

You'll lie to your mother; you'll steal from your dad. When you see their tears, you should feel sad. But you'll forget your morals and how you were raised; I'll be your conscience; I'll teach you my ways. I take kids from parents, and parents from kids; I turn people from God, and separate friends. I'll take everything from you: your looks and your pride. I'll be with you always, right by your side.

You'll give up everything: your family, your home, your friends, your money... and then you'll be alone. I'll take and take, till you have nothing more to give. When I'm finished with you, you'll be lucky to live. If you try me, be warned: this is no game; if given the chance, I'll drive you insane. I'll ravish your body; I'll control your mind. I'll own you completely; your soul will be mine.

The nightmares I'll give you while lying in bed, the voices you'll hear from inside your head. The sweats, the shakes, and the visions you'll see, I want you to know that they're all gifts from me. But then it's too late, and you'll know in your heart, that you are mine, and we shall not part. You'll regret that you tried me, they always do, but you come to me, not I to you.

You knew this would happen, many times you were told, but you challenged my power, and chose to be bold. You could have said no, and just walked away; if you could live that day over, what would you say? I'll be your master, you will be my slave, and I'll even go with you, when you go to your grave. Now that you have met me, what will you do? Will you try me or not? It's all up to you. I can bring you more misery than words can tell; come take my hand, LET ME LEAD YOU TO HELL."
Words of life, my friends. Think about it.
Johnny Wilson, January 10th, 2017

I won't go into all the details of the battle of trying to get Jason help, but what I will say is this: I had to call the police a few times. When they arrived at our place, they told me that the mental health system is messed up and they could only "try" to get him in. I was trying to figure out a way to change this and spoke with a number of mental health professionals as well as Christina to come up with a solid definition of inanimate danger. Then I wrote every Washington State legislator in hopes to get them involved.

This is when I was introduced to NAMI. Senator O'Ban's office directed me to NAMI and told me about Joel's Law, which is a law that he wrote and sponsored. This law was written in hopes to help with this. It is an appeal process that allows families to petition the court when the facilities won't detain an individual. It is a five-day process, which helps, but even with this law it's still difficult because of the lack of beds and facilities.

And let's be honest, if someone is in a bad situation, five days could be too late.

Senator O'Ban told me that the five days was a concession to get the bill passed. There is another law in Washington which would help, but the facilities that take Ricky's Law patients are even fewer. Ricky's Law is directed more toward an individual whose drug or alcohol abuse is out of control, which was the case with my brother. I support both these laws; however, with the lack of facilities. they are not that effective. The state needs to provide the facilities to house those who need the help. So, my work with NAMI will continue.

A.J. Swoboda wrote, "My colleagues in the counseling industry remind me that one of the most important actions someone can undertake who desires emotional healing is to intentionally (under the guidance of trained professionals) remember the trauma and pain-allowing it to become part of the individual's consciousness. Time itself doesn't heal. A part of healing can actually demand revisiting and replaying the pain. Self-knowledge can even play a key role in spiritual conversion as well."[30] This is what I went through. It was truly amazing, reading this now. It took me back to all the sessions that Christina and I had, and facing my past. And if you are struggling, please, please get help!

Here are some statistics on mental health and suicide:

- Suicide is a national public health challenge that causes tremendous pain for individuals, families, and communities across the country.

---

30 Swoboda, A. J. *After Doubt: How to Question Your Faith without Losing It.* Brazos Press, a division of Baker Publishing Group, 2021.

- On average, 132 Americans die by suicide each day, accounting for 47,173 suicide deaths in 2017.
- The number of veteran suicides has exceeded 6,000 each year from 2008-2017.
- Suicide is also the 10th leading cause of death among all ages and the 2nd leading cause of death among those ages 10 to 34 in the United States.

The situation with Jason got so bad I had to move. I had to pull the safety net out from under him. It wasn't a peaceful separation. At 5:00 a.m. one morning, we were in a fight and the police were called one more time as I restrained him from driving drunk. But God had His hands all over it.

I wanted to be out of the situation as soon as possible. I started to look and I found a place that had two apartments available within a week. After speaking with the manager, I filled out the paperwork and moved in the following week. While I was still unpacking, my co-worker and I were talking and she gave me the idea to do a cross wall in my new place. Below is a picture of the wall. You will notice that all of these are crosses; I have no crucifixes on the wall. I did this because Christ was resurrected and is not on the cross. I know that some believe that the crucifix shows the suffering Christ did for us, which I agree with. But for my wall I wanted an empty cross, because of the resurrection power of Christ. (Thank you, Zandi, for inspiring this wall.)

I am currently in one of the best situations I have ever been in and it is a "God Thing." I would not be here without Him being active in my life. Closing Summit, navigating through Covid at the golf club, dealing with Jason's craziness although stressful

The "cross wall" in my home

and frustrating, I knew God would get me through because of seeing Him do it before.

Now, I will not sit here and tell you that I didn't get mad at times and let my temper show toward my brother. A friend called it "godly anger." I did lean on Scotty and the church to get me through this. As I mentioned before, I strongly believe we are made to need one another and it is so rewarding when you see those needs met, and see God work. Your faith can't help but deepen.

I tell people that time in my life was a blessing and it truly was. When it looked as if I had no way out, God provided a way. Even though the way will still cost me over time because of the debt from Summit. I know that God will provide for me, and that I will be able to take care of that in a timely fashion.

I heard this quote in a sermon: "The doorway to failure or success, despair, or hope ultimately opens and closes on the hinges of personal responsibility. Unresolved regret is a malignant tumor growing in your soul. And its only treatment options are to accept personal responsibility for what you have done, and you need to own it, so God can restore you."[31] I believe that this is an ongoing part of life. If you are going to take chances in life, you may regret them if they don't work out. That's okay. My business partner Dusty and I both regret the fact that we didn't leave Lakewood when we truly saw the reality of the books.

That being said, though it's not bad to experience regret, you must resolve it when it happens. Otherwise, it will grow and manifest into something that you won't be able to control.

I've learned that I need to stop trying to control on my own all the negative emotions, thoughts, and impulses I experience. Humans were never designed to be independently "in control," which is counterintuitive to everything I learned (or convinced myself of) in my younger years.

Surrendering control is probably one of the biggest and most significant hurdles I have experienced in my walk with God. And overcoming that hurdle is one of the most powerful of the freedoms I now have in Christ.

RELFECTION or DISCUSSION
Have you been tested by God?

---

31   (McDonald, Sermon from April 11th, 2017)

What was the test and how did you come through it?

Did the test strengthen your faith? If so how?

Do you or someone you know have an addiction and/or had thoughts of suicide?

What can you do to overcome this addiction (or what have you done)? If thoughts of suicide, have you shared this with anyone?

When has someone seen God in you?

Explain how that made you feel.

Chapter Fourteen

SURRENDERING CONTROL

"The Holy Spirit will never fill a man or a woman
who refuses to give up and give over to Him
all control of their entire life."

~ A.W. Tozer

The day I truly gave up control completely was November 22nd when I fell to my knees and cried out to God, "I can't do this!" Since then, the ease of giving things over to God has only grown—small/big/whatever. It's so much easier to give it all over to Him and not worry about the outcome, because it will be what He wants.

Before this revelation, I would have tried to control everything, every aspect. That's how I grew up. After my dad left, my only thought was for what I could do to survive. That was the last thing I held on to because it was about taking care of *me*. (I think that's the biggest fear many people have when they become a Christian—that they will need to give everything up, but those are the things you probably shouldn't have in your life anyway!)

I used to worry about outcomes, and still feel the urge to try to control. But I have learned to give it up and trust God with everything. Take this book, for example. I've given up control. When I made the commitment to finish the book, I said I would write for two hours a day, and I only had five chapters done at the time. But then, in three weeks, it was all done. It was like a flood!

If you are reading this book, and you are in that place of desperation where you are constantly trying to control everything to provide security for yourself, here's what you have to do:

- Let your ego go.
- Humble yourself.
- Place your trust and faith in God, because that's the only way.

Sure, it is tough, but the reward is greater. I want you to understand that when you truly give this up, and the veil is removed, you will see the face of God. As scared as you might be, that's the best decision you could ever make. Just wait and see what God will do with that.

How to Surrender Control

How do you do that? You have to know yourself, which is called "self-awareness." Self-awareness can be cultivated by things like:

1. **Reading (insightful books and Scripture).** I have quoted in this book several of the books and authors that

have been meaningful to me. You, no doubt, will find others that speak to *you*. Also, I recommend you read the Bible in an intentional way, book by book, cover to cover. Eventually it will come together and make sense, especially if you can get yourself into a strong, Bible-teaching church.

2. **Getting to know God (reading the Bible and praying daily).** If you are like me, you will be saying that you don't have time. Make time! It will be the best thing you do. We must sacrifice and give up our life to have this relationship. Prayer along with your reading is where you meet God. God knows our thoughts before we speak, but HE wants to hear us, and HE wants us to hear HIM.

3. **Therapy or counseling.** A professional counselor or pastor can help you examine yourself and then help you ask for forgiveness and seek healing from our Lord. Sin is the biggest roadblock to seeing and experiencing God. Sometimes we need professional help identifying it and weeding it out of our lives.

Author Tony Evans did it for me, driving home 1 Corinthians 10:13, which says, "God can only give you what you can handle; if more, then he will create a path for you." He said that's the only verse in the Bible that is not true (taking it a face value) … God WILL give you more than you can handle, so you will drop to your knees and seek Him! Many people take that verse to mean something it does not. And A.W. Tozer said that God will come *with* you, in such a way that He will make you see the relationship you need to have with Him.

You have to know God (be in the Word, talk to Him). You have to be honest with yourself, with what you've done in your past. Become truthful with yourself: look yourself in the mirror and say, *It's my fault.* That's being humble.

> *"No doubt the first and strongest veils are pride and stubbornness. Nothing is more Adamic in our lives than these. The root of both of these is an inflated opinion of our own selves. That which causes us the most problem is that which we honor the most. One term often used in this regard is the word 'ego.' This one word conveys the root of all of our problems with ourselves, with our families, with our friends, and certainly with our God.*
>
> *It is when we usurp God's rightful place that the trouble occurs. The reason we do that is because we think more highly of ourselves than anybody else, including God. Even if we find ourselves to be wrong, stubbornness will prohibit us from acknowledging that fact, so we cannot press forward. The problem with pride and stubbornness is that they focus on us and obscure the face of God, the One who in all cases provides the solution for our problems. Pride and stubbornness distort the importance of God's authority in our lives."[32]*

Friends (and I'm speaking to men in particular here), we have to learn what being vulnerable is, that we can have vul-

---

32 Tozer, A. W. *Discipleship: What It Truly Means to Be a Christian.* Chicago: Moody Publishers, 2018.

nerability and still be strong. I had to learn this. What is being vulnerable? It is to be capable of being physically or emotionally wounded. And I was not vulnerable for most of my life, as I was afraid of being emotionally wounded. I don't fear this anymore; I know that at some point in my life I will most likely be wounded again. But next time, with my relationship with God and not needing to control the situation anymore, I will come through it for the better.

I believe this is one of the biggest things we face as men in today's society. Most of us are taught from an early age to be rough and tough, strong, and whatever adjective you can think of. Well, I know now that we can be all those things and vulnerable, too.

So, I encourage you to lay down your pride and stubbornness and give up control; you will see the face of God and you will see God do amazing things in your life. I am not going to say that it is easy because it's not! Living for Christ has a cost. The more you get to know God through Scripture and listening for His Spirit directing you, the more you will see what your cost will be. The cost is different for everyone.

The Bible tells us that we have to sacrifice and give up our life to serve Christ. What is this? For me, it's waking up at 4:00 a.m. to read and pray. For you, it might mean not hanging out with some of your friends anymore, or going to places you used to go. These things have certainly been the case for me. These changes become more in focus as the Lord changes your mind and heart.

Trust me when I say that your old self will surface from time to time. What do you do when that happens? For one, don't beat yourself up; you are a child of God and you are growing and maturing. What we need to do, first of all, is repent. In Jeremiah 3, the prophet addresses this by saying, "Return, faithless people; I will cure you of backsliding." And the people reply, "Yes, we will come to you, for you are the Lord our God." A.W. Tozer says this about repentance:

> *"Some have the idea that repentance is to be a drawn-out affair that includes beating yourself down. I think we need to start with repentance, but there comes a time when we need to just turn everything over to God and then not do it anymore. That is the best repentance in the world. If you did something last week you are ashamed of, feel conviction and condemnation about it, and simply say, 'I repent.' Turn it over to the Lord, tell Him about it, and then do not do it anymore."*

The trials that we go through are to strengthen us even if the trial is so hard that you fail. When you look back on the trials, whether you succeed or fail, you will see God's footprints all over them now that you are moving closer to God.

But to get here you have to give up control.

RELFECTION or DISCUSSION

Has control been an issue for you in your life? What has this looked like? (If you answered no, consider: has anyone else ever suggested control might be an issue for you? What did they say it looked like?) Consider if this might be a blind spot for you.

Can you think of a time you were vulnerable with someone, or with God, and experienced healing as a result?

If vulnerability seems like a roadblock, ask God to help you see His care for you, and His understanding of your situation. Ask Him to help you put your guard down with Him and the people closest to you.

Who is God to you? What do you think about Jesus? Is it time to surrender your life to Him?

Chapter Fifteen

DEAR YOUNGER ME

You are holy
You are righteous
You are one of the redeemed
Set apart a brand new heart
You are free indeed
~ Bart Millard

S everal years ago, I saw that the popular Christian band MercyMe was coming to Kent, so I looked for tickets and I found that there was a VIP ticket for two that I could purchase. I was dating Leah at the time, and the show was close to her birthday. This ticket provided us front row seats, backstage access, and an invitation from one of the acts for Leah and me to come on stage to sing her happy birthday. (She wasn't too excited about that because she doesn't like being in front of big crowds, but after it happened, I think she really enjoyed it.)

MercyMe had just released the new album "Welcome to The New," and when I heard the song "Dear Younger Me," it spoke to me in a very interesting and spiritual way. I think the first time I heard this song, I played it over and over so I could let the words sink in, causing me to have deep thoughts about them. I wanted to know the story and inspiration behind them, and the only way to know this was to speak with the man who wrote the song. So, when I saw this VIP ticket package, I couldn't pass it up. I wasn't sure if I would get to meet Bart, but this placed me in a very good situation for that to happen.

A Kindred Spirit in Christ

As Leah and I were waiting to go on stage, we were talking with the group that was to sing "Happy Birthday" and we found out that they were part of a worship team at James McDonald's church. What are the chances of that? It's not chance; it's a "God Thing"! After, they sang happy birthday, we went backstage. When we got backstage, and I was telling them about wanting to meet Bart, they pointed out the MercyMe road manager. I went and introduced myself to him and explained to him why I wanted to meet Bart. He told me that he would be there in about ten minutes, and that he would speak to Bart.

After the band arrived, the manager came and told me that Bart would like to meet. After we introduced ourselves, we sat and shared our testimonies. It was crazy how similar our lives as children were. If you have seen the movie *I Can Only Imagine,* then you know Bart's story growing up. Mine is eerily similar. When we met in 2015, I don't know if Bart knew that the movie was going to be made. But when I saw the movie, it was truly seeing what Bart shared with me that night in Kent come to life.

Back to the song. I asked Bart where the inspiration for this song came from. He told me that his counselor had told him to write a song to his son and tell him what he would tell his younger self. I thought that was an awesome story, another similarity to my own life, with my counselor saying I should write a book. I shared this with him then asked him if I could have permission to use the song and the lyrics. He said, "Yes, you can, as long as I get a copy of the book." (Well, Bart, it has taken some time to finish this and I truly hope you enjoy my book as much as I enjoy your music.)

Bart Millard and me at ShoWare Center,
Kent, Washington March 12, 2015

So, why did I want to use these words to finish my book? Well, I said the words spoke to me, I thought, *Let's close the book with a letter to the younger me.* I couldn't help but think what it would have been like to have had a letter from my older self when I was growing up. And, as I thought of how I was going to use the lyrics in the closing, my first thought was to share them and write my thoughts to them. I am not going to address every line or word, but I want to explain how this song touched me and the reason for including it.

So, here are the lyrics if you don't already know them:[33]

Dear Younger Me,
Where do I start
If I could tell you everything that I have learned so far
Then you could be
One step ahead
Of all the painful memories still running through my head
I wonder how much different things would be
Dear younger me

Hearing this, all I could think was wouldn't that have been nice to know Jesus then the way I know him now. Would the painful memories have been less painful? I wonder if my life would have been any different. I have come to appreciate what A.J. Swoboda wrote: "The message of Jesus is not that he brings answers to the suffering. No. Jesus brings presence to the suffering. He is with them. And it is for that reason, in

---

33 MercyMe Music (ASCAP) / Wet As A Fish Music (Co-Pub) (ASCAP) / (admin at EssentalusicPublishing.com). All right reserved. Used by permission.

our suffering, that we begin to ask deeply profound questions about the nature of the universe. God is right there, suffering alongside us."[34]

I couldn't help but wonder how different things would have been. The painful memories continued until I was able to work through them with Christina and Scotty. I won't say that from time to time that they don't come up, but I am free from the chains that were with them. I suggest to you or anyone you know that is struggling, seek the help of a professional no matter how strong your faith is. Also, find two or more people who are farther along in their walk than you and who you feel you can trust and meet with them so that you can have the help I did during these times.

Dear Younger Me,
I cannot decide
Do I give you a speech about how to get the most out of
your life
Or do I go deep
And try to change
The choices that you'll make 'cuz they're choices that
made me
Even though I love this crazy life
Sometimes I wish it was a smoother ride
Dear younger me, dear younger me

This verse hit home with everything. What I would I say if I was writing "Dear Younger Me"? Would I try to change

---

34   Swoboda A.J, *Messy: God Likes It That Way*, 2012

the choices that I made? I thought about that a long time and the answer would be . . . some of them, yes. There are ones I wouldn't change because they are the ones that I feel have made me who I am.

What Would I Change?

When I was coaching, one of my assistants once told our team, "We have been where you are, you have never been where we are, so listen to us." That is "Dear Younger Me" in a nutshell. I must admit, like most of us, I sometimes wish it was a smoother ride. I think I would share how to have a smoother ride, without changing the craziness in my life. Some of that craziness was fun, and built my faith.

> *If I knew then what I know now*
> *Condemnation would've had no power*
> *My joy, my pain, would've never been my worth*
> *If I knew then what I know now*
> *Would've not been hard to figure out*
> *What I would've changed if I had heard*
> *Dear younger me*
> *It's not your fault*
> *You were never meant to carry this beyond the cross*
> *Dear younger me*

Condemnation would've had no power! Wow, think about that; if you grew up in any way similar to Bart and me, then you understand that. If I had heard "Dear Younger Me," my joy and pain would've never been my worth, and for many, many years that is how I lived: my pain was my worth, and, as you saw, I didn't know what joy was.

Looking back, I know what I would have changed. I don't want to go into the details of those things; however, those of you that knew me before this book likely know the things I would change. Those of you I affected by those things know who you are, and I ask you for your forgiveness. I pray for that forgiveness. I know that some of these things hurt you and others and I am sorry for those choices. They were selfish, and I can honestly say that if I knew then what I know now, I would have never made those choices.

"It's not your fault; you were never meant to carry this beyond the cross." How freeing is that statement? There are things that happen that we cannot control and those are not our fault. But, we end up carrying those things for a lifetime, unless we learn that we can place them at the foot of the cross. This is something we should teach those who are the victims of abuse; it takes a community and church to help people through this.

Let's be clear that this is not condoning things I did in my past; I am sure that Bart would say the same. I believe he is referring to what Paul was talking about in Romans 7:14-21. You were never meant to carry this beyond the cross; none of us were meant to do that. Christ went to the cross so that we don't have to carry our burdens and sin beyond the cross. Our pain, suffering, and scars stop over time when we deepen our walk and faith in the Father.

A.J. Swoboda said, "It is often not the past itself that haunts us but our unwillingness to move past it." I was doing just that for years. I spent ten years in counseling to have the strength to move beyond my past. I can tell you that when you move past your past, it is freeing. This is the hardest thing to do in your walk is to understand that your shame, guilt, resentment, and regret need to be placed on the cross. Jesus took all these things.

This doesn't mean that from time to time you will not see, feel, or think of those things. What it means is that you are free to give them to Jesus so that you are not burdened by them.

You are holy
You are righteous
You are one of the redeemed
Set apart a brand new heart
You are free indeed

Read these five lines again, then read them again, and just one more time. When we accept Christ, we are holy, righteous, one of the redeemed, with a new heart, and we are free indeed. We are broken and redeemed. We receive these when we accept Christ as our savior, but understanding this takes time. As A.J. Swoboda explained it well, "Our gospel forces us to admit that we are wrong and need correction, otherwise, we are following a false gospel. That means there always has to be room in our theology of Jesus for Jesus. We must make room in our understanding of God for God to be God. Otherwise, we are not accepting God for who God is. The rabbis teach that even God is wrestling with the Bible. If you want God to accept you for who you are, you need to accept him for who he is."[35]

---

35   Swoboda, A. J. *Messy: God Likes It That Way*. Grand Rapids, MI: Kregel Publications, 2012.

How do we learn how to accept? Through getting to know the one we are trying to have a relationship with. You can't accept someone in a relationship without knowledge. I recently visited Cairo, Georgia where I was a football coach for two short years. I was on vacation and, during a conversation with Tim Andrews, I decided to make the trip in conjunction with a vacation to Florida. I share this because this trip was a bit of a "God Thing," and you truly sometimes never see the acceptance that people have for you until you sit with them after not seeing them for a while.

I had not been in Cairo in sixteen years, and I must tell you that the trip was truly a blessing— seeing friends, coaches, and players from that season in my life, and being able to catch up and just share stories was amazing. This is where I had my first contact with FCA (Fellowship of Christian Athletes). The mutual acceptance and respect I experienced made me feel very blessed, not only to see these folks but to only have spent two years there and see this was amazing, to see the impact that we had on each other's lives. That helped me grow as a person and a Christian.

Accepting God for Who He Is

So, if part of my letter to my younger self were to include how to accept myself for who I am, it would also have to contain an encouragement to accept God for who *He* is. How do we accept God for God? You have to get to know Him, you have to spend time with Him. To do that, you must also have a community or church to help you develop this knowledge, and you must know yourself.

Every mountain, every valley
Through each heartache you will see

Every moment brings you closer
To whom you were meant to be
Dear younger me, dear younger me

This verse helped me understand that there would still be heartaches and valleys along with the mountains, and all of these are meant to bring us closer to God and who He intended us to be. I have to compare this with what A.J. Swoboda said in *Messy,* "My life is way messier after I started following the Jesus I met than it was before."[36]

We have to understand that when we accept Christ into our life, we will be tested. These tests are to deepen our faith. In the valleys, we can question God, and we can wonder why, but what we cannot do is give up faith. We will never know how long a storm will last, but I can say from experience that the more faith you have and the more you lean into Christ, the easier the storm is to handle.

You are holy
You are righteous
You are one of the redeemed
Set apart a brand new heart
You are free indeed

So, you can see how these lyrics touched me. I left the show in Kent with such an amazing feeling of the Lord being with me. He had his hands on that night and it was truly a "God Thing."

---

36   Swoboda, A. J. *Messy: God Likes It That Way.* Grand Rapids, MI: Kregel Publications, 2012.

My Own Letter to My Younger Self

Dear Younger Me,

Where do I start? There is so much I want to say to you. I really don't know where to start. I don't know what I want to warn you about or what I want to tell you not to change. Some of what you are going to go through is not your fault and it will leave you with scars, both physical and emotional. Don't be afraid because you will make it through. I will tell you to seek help, and don't be afraid to go to counseling. Christina will be one of the best choices you will make (especially if you can seek her out soon than later).

When your MamaDel tells you that God has something special planned for you, believe her and ask her to show you what she means by that. Don't laugh it off. This will help eliminate some of the pain for you and others. Ask her to show you who God is because she knows Him and knows you are redeemed through Him. Do better in school and try to stay out of trouble. Don't be so self-indulgent. I want to tell you to stay away from the drugs and focus on your grades and sports, but I know you won't.

Join the Marines right out of high school don't wait five years. Then, after boot camp, find a mentor to help your faith grow. Scotty Kessler is the one who you want to find. As I write this, I don't know how your life will change; if you do this, only God knows. They say He has a plan for everyone and if my life was His plan, then be safe and know that He is with you through everything you're about to go through.

If I only knew then what I know now . . .

I truly believe there was a reason I went through everything that you are about to go through. It was for His purpose, as John

9:3 says, "This happened so that the power of God could be seen in him." I still feel that I am not who I should be or where I should be, and I still wonder why me. It's like Pastor Martin said: "Is it how God chooses the unlikeliest people to accomplish God's desires for the world." I am definitely one of the unlikeliest people for this.

"When we speak poorly to ourselves about ourselves, we fail to take seriously what Christ says over us as His beloved. We are loved by Jesus. Truth be told, if we had friends or family members who talked to us the same way we often talk down to ourselves, we might very well be able to categorize that as abuse. Self-abuse is never the geography of healthy spiritual formation. That said, the more we begin to walk in the presence of Christ, the more we become aware of the false self and the sin that lurks in our souls. Often, the closer we come to Jesus, the further Jesus feels from us. The light really does illuminate the darkness. We do not overcome the darkness of the self by beating up the self."- A.J. Swoboda

Remember this and don't be so hard on yourself as you grow up. Even as I write this book, I am moving closer and closer to God. My thoughts and behaviors are being molded into my obedience to God's Word. I used to hate myself and beat myself up all the time, but looking back from where I am now, I can forgive my old self. That is something that was hard to do, but as Scripture says, we have to forgive because we have been forgiven. This means we must forgive ourselves, too.

I want you to be vulnerable and honest to those who love you. I didn't do this. I covered up the past and hid it from those around me for too long. So, accept yourself for who you are and let people in. Know that love comes with a cost and if you love, you will get hurt. The ones you love will leave either by death or by choice, but don't let this stop you from loving! I just want you to know it's okay to give yourself—ALL of you—to someone. Understand that some of the people who will shape your faith will fall. We are all humans, and we are not perfect. But we must understand that we still need to show others love, even when they fall because—like you—they have sin in them. I want you always remember the Paradoxical Commandments that are listed below and live by these words in everything you do:

People are unreasonable, illogical, and self-centered.
Love them anyway.
If you do good, people will accuse you of selfish, ulterior motives.
Do good anyway.
If you are successful, you will win false friends and true enemies.
Succeed anyway.
The good you do today will be forgotten tomorrow.
Do good anyway.
Honesty and frankness make you vulnerable.
Be honest and frank anyway.
The biggest people with the biggest ideas can be shot down by the smallest people with the smallest minds.
Think big anyway.
People favor underdogs but follow only top dogs.
Fight for the underdog anyway.

What you spend years building may be destroyed over-night.
Build anyway.
People really need help but may attack you if you help them.
Help people anyway.
Give the world the best you've got, and you'll get kicked in the teeth.
Give the world the best you've got anyway.
(Dr. Kent Keith, 1968, 2001)

Remember that you are a child of God, and you are loved, even though there will be times in your life you don't feel love. You are redeemed and you are made holy because of the cross. You were never meant to carry this beyond the cross. And know that God is waiting for you, and when you finally come home you will be made new, and you will be set free. I hope this helps you have a smoother ride. Learn from me because you have never been where I am now, and where you will end up is the best place I have ever been: in our Father's arms. James McDonald said in his book, Act Like a Man, *"If you don't love more and better than you used to, you are not [saved] walking in faith." I changed the ending of that quote from "saved" to "walking in faith." The reason is that you are saved no matter what you do. But if you love more and better than you used to, you are walking in faith. I can honestly say that I love more and better than I used to.*
Blessings to you my son,
An Older John

Embracing the Brokenness, Living in Redemption
I know God's not finished; this I believe. This is just the start of what God has planned for me. As MamaDel said, "Johnny, God has something special planned for you." I truly believe this now, and I know He has something special for you, too.

Remember: there are two sides of brokenness. There is the sadness of being broken—meaning that someone, something, or an event, causes this sadness, confusion, shame, guilt, or PTSD. This kind of brokenness leaves you feeling alone and condemned, which is the heartache of the world. But the other side of brokenness, the blessed side, is where you have moved close enough to God that through the grace and power of His Spirit you are broken in a way that you see yourself in light of that grace and love. This is the brokenness that leads us to our redemption.

God loves the broken; just read Psalm 139. God "breaks" us from our old life; this blessed brokenness is a beautiful journey that moves us closer to Him and to a Christlike life.

I pray you find that side of brokenness, and that it leads you to the Father God who is waiting with open arms to redeem you and welcome you to His family.

"God made us without our permission but will not save
us without our consent.
We have to be open to being healed and saved."
~A.J. Swoboda

RELFECTION or DISCUSSION
What are your thoughts on the Paradoxical Commandments? How can you implement them into your daily life?

What are your thoughts about the "Dear Younger Me" lyrics by MercyMe?

Have you or do you know someone who has had negative self-talk? If so, what can or did you do to change that? How could you help someone through this?

How have you experienced brokenness in your life? Think of ways you can see God's redemption in it. Take time to pray and ask Him to reveal more of how He wants to work in your life through it.

Write a letter to your "younger me."

Recommended Reading

Basham, Don: *Deliver Us from Evil: A Pastor's Reluctant Encounters with the Powers of Darkness.*

Evans, Tony: *Detours: The Unpredictable Path to Your Destiny*

Ingram, Chip: *The Invisible War: What Every Believer Needs to Know about Angels, Demons, and Spiritual Warfare*

Marlantes, Karl: *What It Is Like to Go to War*

Martin, James: *Jesus: A Pilgrimage*

McDonald, James: *Act Like Men: 40 Days to Biblical Manhood*

McDonald, James: *Living in a Place Called Repentance*

Swoboda, A.J.: *Redeeming How We Talk*

Swoboda, A.J.: *After Doubt: How to Question Your Faith without Losing It*

Swoboda, A.J.: *Messy: God Likes It That Way*

Swoboda, A.J.: *A Glorious Dark: Finding Hope in The Tension Between Belief and Experience*

Swoboda, A.J.: *The Dusty Ones: Why Wandering Deepens Your Faith*

Tozer, A.W.: *The Pursuit of God*

Tozer, A.W.: *The Crucified Life: How to Live Out a Deeper Christian Experience*

ABOUT THE AUTHOR

J ohn Jarman is a U.S. Marine Corps veteran who served during Operation Desert Storm and holds a Master of Science in Physical Education/Athletic Administration from Ohio University. After coaching and teaching for 17 years, John transitioned to a career in the fitness industry. John started his own company, Summit Strength & Conditioning, and was the owner and operator for seven years until the Covid-19 pandemic hit. Now, John is the Fitness Director at Fircrest Golf Club in Washington State, where he specializes in golf-specific training. He is also continuing in his pursuit of a Master of Theology at Faith International University, and is involved in Men's

Discipleship in his local church in Tacoma, Washington. He is a member of the Club Spa & Fitness Association, Washington Fitness Alliance, and the National Alliance on Mental Illness. *www.brokenandredeemed.com*

A free ebook edition is available with the purchase of this book.

To claim your free ebook edition:

1. Visit MorganJamesBOGO.com
2. Sign your name CLEARLY in the space
3. Complete the form and submit a photo of the entire copyright page
4. You or your friend can download the ebook to your preferred device

Print & Digital Together Forever.

Snap a photo   Free ebook   Read anywhere

CPSIA information can be obtained
at www.ICGtesting.com
Printed in the USA
JSHW040241150722
28145JS00001B/23